Oxfordshire Graves and Gravestones

Marilyn Yurdan

Sir Francis Page's monument in Steeple Aston church. At his side rests his second wife, Frances. Page acquired the reputation of a hanging judge and legend says that the widows, in the form of owls, of the 100 men that he hanged during his career chase him in a beer barrel up and down Middle Aston pond. The monument was erected at his own expense. (Newsquest Oxfordshire)

Oxfordshire Graves and Gravestones

Marilyn Yurdan

First published 2010

The History Press
The Mill, Brimscombe Port
Stroud, Gloucestershire, GL5 2QG
www.thehistorypress.co.uk

British Library Cataloguing in Publication Data.
A catalogue record for this book is available from the British Library.

ISBN 978 0 7524 5257 9

Typesetting and origination by The History Press
Printed in India, Aegean Offset
Manufacturing managed by Jellyfish Print Solutions Ltd

Contents

Acknowledgements

Thanks are due to John Brown, Chris McDowell, and Newsquest Oxfordshire Picture Library, which supplied a great number of the pictures in this book for which the author is extremely grateful.

Signwriter and painter Colin Dundas of Loughton, Milton Keynes, renewing the lettering on Barrie Edmond's gravestone in Thame churchyard.

Introduction

Oxfordshire as covered by this book is the present county, which after the boundary changes of 1974 now includes the Vale of White Horse, formerly part of Berkshire. Although Oxfordshire has no vast urban necropolis, it contains within its boundaries a whole range of different types of burial site, many of them fascinating. Some are situated within the boundaries of present communities while others are to be found well away from built-up areas.

Seemingly random burials are to be found all over the county. Most of these are tribal and family plots such as those dating from Neolithic to Saxon times, which have been discovered all over the Abingdon area. Others, who were interred away from conventional sites, are suicides, murder victims and criminals.

The British practice of burying the dead in churches and graveyards at the heart of the community is an unusual one and dates only from the Middle Ages. The walled burial grounds seen outside towns and villages in Europe had no equivalent in Britain until the opening of the municipal cemeteries from the mid-nineteenth century onwards. Even today, smaller plots as close to the ancient graveyards as possible are chosen as extensions by parish councils rather than larger new ones further away.

Minster churches date back to Anglo-Saxon times when they acted as mother churches to a large area and had a number of satellite churches over which they had burial rights. The title minister is not synonymous with cathedral although a small number of them serve the same purpose today, notably York Minster. These rights meant that those who died within its control had to be brought to the minster churchyard for burial, for which a fee was payable. There have been instances of disgraceful scenes in which corpses were seized on the way to a grave in a local churchyard and taken off to the minster burial ground. With the rise of the parish system in late-Saxon days, the influence of the minsters declined and they eventually became no more than large parish churches. Today, former minsters can often be identified by the burial grounds which surround them, normally oval in shape and

Many ancient English churches have lychgates at the entrance to the churchyard like this one at Didcot. *Līc* is the Old English word for corpse and coffins were set down on benches under the gate to await the priest who would lead the funeral procession towards the church. (Newsquest Oxfordshire)

unusually large for the size of the community. Oxfordshire minster churches include Bampton and Shipton-under-Wychwood.

The first generation or two of those affected by the closure of the ancestral parish churchyards may well have been distressed by the fact that they themselves would not be allowed to lie near their forebears and friends. The familiar higgledy-piggledy old churchyards where they had played as children must have seemed much less intimidating than the orderly modern ones. On a more practical level, they might have to travel a considerable distance to place flowers and tend graves if their loved ones ended up in one of the larger municipal cemeteries.

Inside the church, early medieval tombs may bear heraldic devices, which give information about the incumbent rather than his or her name. The earliest form of memorial was a plain slab with a cross incised into it; the majority of these date from the twelfth century, although there are a few examples of earlier ones. About a century later recumbent effigies appeared and remained popular for centuries. These monuments give a great deal of valuable information about clothing, jewellery, footwear, hairstyles, armour and weapons of the time.

These modern calvary-type markers are in the burial ground at Burford Priory. The residents of this Anglican Benedictine house moved out in November 2008 when the priory was sold to Matthew Freud and his wife, Rupert Murdoch's daughter, Elisabeth, for £6.5 million. (Newsquest Oxfordshire)

The parish churchyard at Ardington with a Victorian 'knight in armour' in the foreground. (Newsquest Oxfordshire)

Memorial brasses can be found from the late-thirteenth century onwards, the golden age being the later Middle Ages, although some fine Victorian examples exist, usually in cathedrals and larger churches where they commemorate bishops and other high-ranking clergymen. England is particularly rich in brasses, some 10,000 of them surviving, and many fine specimens can be found in Oxfordshire.

The poorest parishioners went to their graves outside in the churchyard, sometimes just in their shrouds in a reusable coffin placed on the parish bier, or carried by members of their family and neighbours. Carts were also used and farmers would often be conveyed in one of their own wagons. Shrouds rather than coffins were the norm until the late-seventeenth century, although shrouds continued to be used until the twentieth century.

Although the graves of ordinary people were not usually marked with names and details until the seventeenth century, gravestones did exist for we read of them being stolen. In the Middle Ages markers were often made of wood. Sometimes these were crosses similar to those which are occasionally found to this day, others

A typical Cotswold bale tomb (that of the White family of Witney), showing a bale of wool coupled with a skull symbolizing mortality.

of a type called head-boards, since they resembled bed-heads, or leaping-boards because they were just the right height to be jumped over by disrespectful youths. Such boards lasted into Victorian times as can be seen in sentimental paintings of funerals, but wooden memorials in general fell from favour because they rotted and made the churchyard look untidy.

In a typical churchyard, the oldest and most prestigious graves were to the south side of the church. The north side, usually in the shadow of the church building, was originally reserved for suicides (if they were buried in consecrated ground at all) and those who had not been baptised.

In an article which appeared in the *Oxfordshire Family Historian*, volume 1, number 4, Spring 1978, Pamela Keegan notes that in the small village of Cropredy to the north of the county:

> ... a pattern emerged of trade groups. To the west of the tower are many Butchers and Farmers. On a triangular patch to the south, a family of Plumbers and Glaziers predominate.

A line of Harness-makers are near the south porch and further south-east a large area of Millers, backed to the east by Yeomen. On the north side are the Cordwainers and Wheelwrights. The former families are opposite their family house in Red Lion Street and the latter are relatives and descendants of the innkeeper of the Red Lion Inn.

The fact that these parishioners are buried near to each other may of course be due to the fact that they were related by blood or marriage rather than merely because they shared occupations.

Older headstones vary from region to region depending on the material most readily available, the traditional Oxfordshire ones being of the local limestone but in more recent times the choice has increased considerably. According to the website of the Church of SS Mary and John in Oxford's Cowley Road, which was consecrated in 1878, the range of materials used for gravestones in this relatively modern churchyard is vast. It includes 'Italian marble, grey Cornish granite, pink and red Scottish granite, Ancaster stone, Bramley Fall sandstone, Clipsham stone, Delabole Devonian slate from Cornwall, Forest of Dean stone, Hopton Wood stone, Penryhn slate, Portland stone, York stone and, of course, Blue Hornton stone.' Worthy of note are the terracotta stones made of material similar to Coade stone made by local firm, Thomas Grimsley & Sons. At one time many of the graves were surrounded by iron railings but these were stolen in the 1920s and '30s and sold for scrap. Four metal crosses survive as well as several decaying wooden memorials. Old gravestones show symbols portraying the brevity of human life, notably skulls and skeletons, hour-glasses to represent the sands of time, and snakes biting their own tails forming the circle of life. Other, much less common, grave-markers are cast-iron crosses, early twentieth-century examples of which can be found at Stoke Talmage and wooden crosses and calvaries.

The need for large municipal cemeteries increased in the mid-nineteenth century due to an increase in population which led to the ancient parish graveyards becoming over full and in some cases amounting to health hazards. The situation had been made worse by the series of epidemic diseases (of which cholera in 1832, 1849 and 1854 was only one example), which swept the country and sometimes resulted in a need for mass graves. A graphic example is given by the Revd W.R. Browell, Fellow of Pembroke College, Oxford, who wrote on 21 September 1832 concerning the crowded state of St Aldate's churchyard, which adjoins the college. He complained that whenever a grave was opened several coffins came to light. An officiating clergyman 'was witness to an indecent exposure of this kind which was very distressing'. Even the pathways in the churchyard had been dug up to provide more burial-space, and had the unpleasant habit of caving in under the passer-by when a coffin lid gave way. The sexton was forced to probe the ground with a long iron rod before attempting to dig a new grave, 'with a violence and disrespect to

The churchyard at Bampton showing the extent to which centuries of burial have raised the level of the ground.

Non-conformist churches and chapels as well as parish ones have fascinating old graveyards. This remote Baptist church at Cote was founded in 1656, although the present building dates from 1739. Its newer extension is still open for burials. (Newsquest Oxfordshire)

the remains of the dead revolting to our sense of propriety.' Revd Browell stressed that St Aldate's was not the only central Oxford parish to have a graveyard in such a dreadful state as those of St Ebbe (with more than 3,000 residents), and of St Peter le Bailey, St Michael, All Saints, St Mary Magdalen, and, in particular, Carfax, were disgraceful, and their clergy all 'at a loss' to know how to improve matters. He closes with the hope that Oxford will soon get its much-needed cemetery. Unfortunately, as a clergyman he was very much in the minority, and so this wish was not to be fulfilled for a considerable time.

Over-burying continued to be both controversial and a hazard to health. Despite unrelenting efforts by Oxford City Council in 1839, 1842 and 1847 to establish a municipal cemetery away from the centre, it was not until 1855 when Orders in Council were issued forbidding new burial grounds within the city limits that any progress was made. These stipulated that burials in Oxford should be discontinued in all of the ancient churchyards, with the exception of existing vaults or walled graves which still had vacancies. Other exceptions were the graveyards of the city's Roman Catholic, Baptist, Wesleyan, and Congregational chapels, those belonging to the Workhouse and the Radcliffe Infirmary, and the burial plot in the castle gaol. There was also a burial ground attached to the County Pauper Lunatic Asylum at Littlemore.

As individual churchyards became full, a series of Acts were passed in order to deal with the problem until, in 1857, a nation-wide system of public cemeteries was established. Parish officials set up their own Burial Boards which were charged with making provision for the burial of the dead of the parish. This they could do by opening a cemetery which was to be paid for by Poor Rate contributions. Burial Boards were responsible for the management and upkeep of the cemetery and the sale of the grave plots in it.

In 1876, however, the Cemetery Committee of the Local Board at Oxford reported that the orders of 1855 could not be complied with, and that St Thomas's and St Clement's churchyards were still in occasional use. As a result, the Local Board was constituted a Burial Board, and negotiations began with Christ Church regarding the purchase of land at Rose Hill. Two years later the churchyard of St Mary and St John in Cowley Road was consecrated, which went some way towards improving the problem in East Oxford at least.

There are more than 170,000 Commonwealth war graves in the United Kingdom, the majority being those of service personnel who were killed in action or in training accidents or died from wounds or infections. Oxford (Botley) cemetery, which was initially intended for the graves of casualties of the First World War, was later extended and designated a Royal Air Force regional cemetery for the use of RAF stations in Berkshire and the adjoining counties during the Second World War.

Not all war graves are to be found in special cemeteries, some being in home parish churchyards where they are to be found singly or in small groups, mostly identified by the distinctive neat headstone, although some have private memorials. In all more than 12,000 churchyards and cemeteries contain war graves. For example, the one at SS Mary and John in Oxford has thirteen of these, the maintenance of which is paid for by the Commonwealth War Graves Commission.

By the middle of the twentieth century most of Oxford's Victorian cemeteries had themselves become filled. New cemeteries were attached to some, but not all, of the churches which were opened during the nineteenth century. Most of these were destined to be short-lived. St John the Baptist in Summertown, for example, opened in 1832 and closed in 1896 when a letter from the Council Office, Whitehall, ordered that burials be 'discontinued forthwith and entirely.' St John's was replaced by the new Church of St Michael in 1909 and was demolished in 1924.

Victorian burial grounds have received differing treatment, the majority continuing to be well-tended. Osney is a notable exception as it has for the most part been allowed to revert to a wild state and dogs are walked among the isolated gravestones which do remain.

Municipal cemeteries are found only in Oxford and the larger towns, it being preferred to increase burial space piecemeal. These are non-denominational, and by no means exclusively for the use of Christians. There are sections for Jewish burials and for those of other religions, although Muslims are not well represented as most prefer to be buried in their ancestral towns and villages.

In addition to the Church of England graveyards, old and new, and their extensions, there are many small plots all over Oxfordshire which belonged to Roman Catholic churches, Non-conformist chapels, workhouses, hospitals and asylums. Most of the urban non-Anglican places of worship have never had a burial ground and some of those that did exist have been deconsecrated, usually because the site has been converted for a secular purpose such as conversion into houses and gardens.

Local historians have undertaken the time-consuming task of recording memorial inscriptions in churches and graveyards all over the county. Their findings can be consulted in local history collections including the Centre for Oxfordshire Studies above the Westgate Library in Oxford, and the County Record Office at Cowley. However, due to the ongoing effects of weather and pollution, inclusion in these records cannot guarantee that the inscription, or indeed the headstone itself, is still in existence.

Another feature of both churchyards and cemeteries is the family vault in which several generations can be buried before it is finally sealed up. Vaults are frequently constructed with bricks and may be accessed from either the interior of the church or the burial ground outside.

As regards modern graves, what is allowed to be written on the gravestone and placed on the grave itself varies enormously from place to place. Some authorities (usually incumbents of old churchyards) are very strict, while others permit the bereaved to express their feelings in the most uninhibited way. Today's stones come in an impressive range of sizes, colours and designs: from black granite to glistening white marble, with swans, flowers, sunsets and, increasingly, include a picture of the deceased, something previously restricted largely to Roman Catholic headstones.

Historically, grave goods accompanying a burial generally indicate a pagan burial and the practice of providing the deceased with a variety of items which they might need in the next life died out with the spread of Christianity. However, in the last decade or so the phenomenon of what might be called modern grave goods has made its appearance in both cemeteries and churchyards. This seems to relate more frequently to male burials and takes the form of putting on the grave virtually anything which gave the occupant pleasure in life. Boys' graves may be adorned with toys and miniature cars, planes or tanks, and older men's with signs reading 'Gone Fishing', or burrowing moles or Jack Russell terriers. It is the graves of young men, though, which attract the most attention, with offerings ranging from the more usual poems, photographs and lanterns to unopened cans of lager, cigars in tubs and even football scarves. In their own way, the graves of today have become a feature of our Oxfordshire churchyards and cemeteries.

A highly-decorated modern grave in Wolvercote municipal cemetery.

The memorials belonging to these plots for the burial of ashes at Wolvercote cemetery come in a variety of shapes, sizes and materials.

A practise which continued to provoke protest and revulsion for decades, cremation, was made legal and began to become more common at the end of the nineteenth century. Its critics believed that mortal remains should be available for reassembly when the last trump sounds. Oxford Crematorium opened in Bayswater Lane, now part of Headington, but at that time part of Stanton St John, in 1939; the county's second crematorium opened at Banbury in 1962.

Ashes are disposed of by relatives in a number of ways, some being left in the charge at the crematorium and others being taken to be scattered in places which were dear to the deceased in his or her lifetime. In addition, a sensible compromise between interment and cremation has evolved in the burial of the ashes in churchyards and cemeteries. Most old churchyards have a section of miniature graves complete with memorial stones, which can be decorated with flowers and wreaths.

Finally, a reminder that last resting places may not always be where they seem to be. Despite the fact that burial registers and memorials may combine to prove that an individual was indeed buried at a certain place on a certain date this does not mean that he or she necessarily remained there. Family chapels have been rebuilt and even removed; tombs have been repositioned to the extent that in some cases information regarding the exact whereabouts of the remains of well-known people has been lost. This is particularly true regarding religious foundations which closed as part of the Dissolution of the Monasteries in the 1530s when their churches were demolished. One notable example is Abingdon Abbey, the site of which contained the bones of many distinguished persons, including members of the royal family and nobility.

This rearrangement of remains is also true of the parish church and has been happening for centuries. Pepys's experience in his family's parish church of St Olave, Hart Street, cannot have been unique. In March 1664 he met the grave-maker to choose a place for his brother,

> to lie in, just under my mother's pew. But to see how a man's tombes are at the mercy of such a fellow, that for sixpence he would (as his owne words were), 'I will justle them together, but I will make room for him;' speaking of the fullness of the middle isle where he was to lie.

A series of old gravestones belonging to several generations of the Ivings family, which have been sympathetically re-grouped in the churchyard at Sandford St Martin.

Some old churchyards had a construction called a charnel-house, which was built for the storage of bones which had been disturbed during alterations to the church or when fresh graves were being dug. Some places still have such structures which are used today for less macabre purposes such as storing gardening tools.

In addition, the recent repositioning of old gravestones for convenience in keeping the burial ground tidy has taken place all over the country, on some occasions provoking great criticism. Stones are to be found in various venues: placed against the church, propped up against the walls of the churchyard and in extreme cases set into pathways. One parish which has moved gravestones for a very worthwhile reason is Stanford in the Vale, where interesting memorials of historical significance have been taken inside the church for protection.

Unmarked Graves

Oxfordshire has a variety of burial places, ranging in date from prehistoric to early modern times, in which the graves are unmarked. Some are among the most important archaeological sites in the country which were in use for centuries, but dozens more graves came to light by accident, usually during the course of building work. We shall never know the names of those who built or occupied them.

In Tudor and Stuart days the northern part of Oxfordshire was noted for its barrows, the majority of which have since been ploughed up. However, aerial photographs show traces of barrows all over the county, many of which have been excavated.

A section of a Neolithic stone barrow excavated at Ascott-under-Wychwood was reconstructed in the County Museum. About fifty skeletons were found, most having died in their twenties and some showing signs of a disability similar to spina bifida.

One barrow which has its own legend attached to it lies off the Ridgeway, near Ashbury. This is Wayland's Smithy, named after a character in Northern European mythology who learned his trade from the trolls. In his novel, *Kenilworth*, Sir Walter Scott relates how a traveller, who tied his up his horse outside the smithy and left a coin on the capstone, would come back in the morning to find it newly shod.

In reality Wayland's Smithy is what is left of a large-chambered long barrow which was used for burial by several generations. Radio-carbon dating dates it from between 3700 and 3400 BC. It was excavated in 1919 and again in 1962-3, when it was shown to have been constructed at two different periods. First to be built was a wooden chamber with a stone floor where the remains of at least fourteen skeletons were found. The bodies would have been in varying stages of decomposition when they were put in position, following the practice of exposing bodies to the elements before final burial. At a later date a long mound with chambers was built above the

This photograph shows archaeologists measuring a bone found in a Stone-Age long barrow at Ascott-under-Wychwood in September 1968. Human bones such as these provided clues about life some 5,000 years ago. The find was the climax of three years' excavation on the site, carried out under the auspices of the Ministry of Public Building and Works and the Oxford City and County Museum. It was directed by the museum's field officer, Don Benson, and was one of the most comprehensive Neolithic excavations in the country to date. The bones showed that about twenty people had been buried in the barrow. They were piled in stone cists and were difficult to examine and sort; it was also thought that the corpses had not been interred immediately after death but had been allowed to decompose. (Newsquest Oxfordshire)

first barrow and this contained eight skeletons. After the last burials, these chambers were filled with rubble and the site abandoned.

The Barrow Hills site on the borders of Abingdon and Radley supports Abingdon's claim to be the oldest continuously-inhabited town in the country. There has been both a prehistoric and a Roman cemetery on the Barrow Hills site but the barrows themselves date from the Bronze Age. In the case of Barrow Hills the Home Secretary specified that the remains 'should be placed in suitable containers, conveyed to a laboratory for purposes of scientific study and on completion conveyed to the Ashmolean Museum, Oxford, for storage.' The main question asked by the people making up the crocodile of visitors at the Open Day was what happens to the bodies? David Miles wrote in October 1984:

> It is a criminal offence (albeit one which will cost you no more than £25) to remove any body or part of a body or cremated remains without lawful authority. Authority comes in the form of a Home Office Licence costing £10 and signed by the Home Secretary.

The licence states: 'The removal shall be effected with due care and attention to decency'.

The first excavations to be carried out at Dorchester-on-Thames, in 1962, showed evidence of a Belgic settlement, but in addition a small Roman town of some 13.6 acres (5.5 ha) was found to lay to the west of the modern village, between the High Street and Watling Street. Most of this is covered by present-day Dorchester and the allotment to the west of the abbey. It survived into the early fifth century and may have been the home of a Roman garrison, although later in the century it was occupied by Saxons. Among the graves discovered there was one which contained the skeleton of a Roman child wearing hobnailed boots in which he could walk into the next world. Other Roman remains include a burial ground at Stratton Audley, on Akeman Street, and in the churchyard at Burford is a Roman sarcophagus which was almost certainly brought from elsewhere.

Although the Saxons seldom lived in of what survived of previous settlements, they certainly made use of them to bury their dead. One example of this is Blewburton Hill, near Blewbury, which dates from the Iron Age but was later used by the Saxons for family burials.

When the Saxton Road development was built in the 1930s in south Abingdon, a large Anglo-Saxon cemetery was unearthed, itself constructed near Bronze Age barrows. Pottery and metal work dating from the beginning of the fifth century was found. The first Saxons practised cremation, the ashes being placed into urns which were then buried; there was a high percentage of cremations to burials. Grave goods, often toilet sets, were found and pottery made for funerary not domestic use and there were many bronze brooches on the site. The Saxton Road Anglo-Saxon cemetery was in use for several centuries and includes both pagan and Christian burials. It was the largest of numerous Saxon sites of various dates from all over the Abingdon area.

In March 1975, the Amey Roadstone Corporation gave a second annual payment of £7,500 to the Oxford Archaeological Unit to help with its work in the Upper Thames Valley, where they had been excavating Iron Age, Roman and Saxon sites on Corporation-owned property. The most significant find was a pagan Saxon cemetery of a hundred graves at the Wally Corner gravel pit near Berinsfield. With the remains were personal possessions including spears, shields, knives and buckets with the male skeletons, and brooches, necklaces, cosmetic items and spinning apparatus with the female ones. Traces of textiles and wood were taken to be analyzed at the Ashmolean Museum. The Unit planned to uncover what was left of a Saxon village near the burial site. (Newsquest Oxfordshire)

Opposite: About thirty skeletons were unearthed in a field at Coral Springs, Curbridge when the new Witney by-pass was under construction in 1975. Archaeologists from the Oxfordshire Archaeological Unit were uncertain whether the remains dated from late-Roman or Saxon times. There had been an extensive Roman settlement, complete with cemetery, in the area. The children watching a skeleton being brushed up are from the Batt Church of England Primary School, Witney. (Newsquest Oxfordshire)

In the 1970s the remains of a sixth-century warrior were found at Radley Road in Abingdon, which proved that the site was still occupied after the Romans had deserted the villa which had been built nearby. (Newsquest Oxfordshire)

Opposite: Two Anglo-Saxon skeletons, one male and one female, were found by the Oxfordshire Archaeological Unit at Wally Corner, Berinsfield in 1975. They were found on what was thought to be a pagan Saxon cemetery dating from about AD 400, which was first excavated when ninety-nine skeletons and three cremations were discovered. (Newsquest Oxfordshire)

The University of Oxford's Botanic Garden was founded as a physic garden by Henry Danvers, Earl of Danby. In 1621 he purchased the lease of 5 acres of meadowland called Paris Mead just outside the city limits for £250. The site had been the Jewish burial ground for generations until the Jews were expelled from England in 1290. When the foundations for the garden's boundary wall were dug in 1630 cartloads of bones were removed and later, when bulwarks were thrown up for the defence of Magdalen Bridge in 1642, more skeletons were disturbed. (Newsquest Oxfordshire)

Opposite from top:
In December 1968 two 1,200-year-old skeletons were found in shallow graves at New Wintles Farm, near Eynsham. They were believed to be that of a woman and a child. The adult had a disc brooch at each shoulder and an iron chain around her neck. Both skeletons, which were found at a distance from each other, belong to the middle-to-late Saxon period. They were discovered by Margaret Gray, a freelance archaeologist, and her team of seven helpers. (Newsquest Oxfordshire)

This Anglo-Saxon girl died when she was about 18 and was buried in gravel near Dorchester-on-Thames. She was wearing gilded bronze brooches and a necklace of amber beads. (Newsquest Oxfordshire)

The site of Eynsham Abbey, which was founded in the eleventh century, yielded more than thirty skeletons during excavations in 1971. They were believed to date from the early eleventh to the thirteenth centuries; the idea of a mass grave was refuted as the bodies had been buried at different times. One of the directors of the dig thought that the site formed part of a parish cemetery situated just outside the abbey walls. (Newsquest Oxfordshire)

In the spring of 2008 the media was full of reports of a number of skeletons found at St John's College during the construction of a new quadrangle. Three archaeologists spent several weeks working at a site in Blackhall Road, off St Giles. The remains were thought to be those of executed criminals or men killed in battle, and said to be one of the city's most important finds for about fifty years. They were in a mass grave and all clothing had been removed before burial.

Sean Wallis, project manager for Thames Valley Archaeological Services, said that his team was expecting to find proof of activity from medieval times, but no bodies.

The skeletons were estimated to be of men in their late teens who had been executed in the Saxon period. They were in a good state of preservation but appeared to have been thrown into the ground on top of each other rather than having been given an orderly Christian burial. The other remarkable feature was that the corpses had not been buried immediately after death but had been stored until they had started to decay.

The county's abbeys, monasteries and other foundations provided a final resting-place for influential people, including royalty and nobility, who wished to be buried in a religious setting as they believed that this would speed up their arrival in heaven. Along with a large number of nameless monks and servants, their graves are now unmarked and unaccounted for but still occasionally come to light.

A burial site covering several centuries was discovered in Abingdon near the Abbey Grounds. The first skeletons to come to light were from the Middle Ages and one from Roman times. The medieval skeletons were 2–3ft below ground and underneath them were the Roman skeletons, together with traces of what was believed to be a Roman building. The bones were in good condition, having been preserved by the soil. Assessment was being carried out by the Oxfordshire Archaeology Unit when this photograph was taken in February 1987. (Newsquest Oxfordshire)

About fifteen so-called 'Cloister Skeletons' were discovered at Christ Church in Oxford in 1985. (Newsquest Oxfordshire)

Opposite from top:
Mr R. Bradshaw is shown with just a few of the human bones found in Oxford High Street in 1958 when new GPO lines were being put down outside the University Church of St Mary the Virgin. The vicar believed that the remains were almost certainly earlier than the fourteenth century. (Newsquest Oxfordshire)

Mr T. Harnett poses with a skull found in Alfred Street, Oxford in 1962. Along with other bones, it came from the burial ground of St Edward's, an ancient church which is known to have existed by 1122 but which closed in the early fifteenth century. (Newsquest Oxfordshire)

Above, left: On the eve of the Oxfordshire Archaeology Unit's last day at the site of Blackfriars Priory in St Ebbes, Oxford, in 1974, a stone coffin was discovered. The director, Humphrey Woods, stated that it belonged to a person of high status, either a benefactor or one of the priors. The lid had been taken, possibly for sale as a paving slab after the Reformation, but the skeleton remained inside the coffin. The man was tall and had been buried with his arms folded over his chest. (Newsquest Oxfordshire)

Above, right: In 1976 the rector of Wallingford, the Revd Denis Janes, was called upon to re-bury the remains of more than thirty people in a mass grave at St Leonard's churchyard. These citizens had been buried some seven centuries ago in the churchyard of St Michael's Church, which closed in around 1340. The skeletons had been unearthed two years previously by a team from the town's Historical and Archaeological Society. (Newsquest Oxfordshire)

Opposite top, from left:
A mysterious find made in Stert Street, Abingdon, in 1975 was the skeleton of a baby which had been buried under a medieval house. Shown are Bob Wilson and Mike Parrington (right), Vale of White Horse field officer of the Oxfordshire Archaeology Unit, told local press that the discovery was a riddle. The child may have been part of a foundation ritual, a murder victim, or unbaptised and therefore ineligible for Christian burial. (Newsquest Oxfordshire)

This skull belonged to a man in his thirties who died in Banbury during the Civil War. His remains were found on the castle site during archaeological excavations in 1972. The skull, shown here with assistant site archaeologist Richard Chambers, was examined by a dentist who claimed that in life, 'He had a filthy mouth, with bleeding gums and bad breath which was probably normal for the period.' (Newsquest Oxfordshire)

A single trench dug for the foundations of a new office block behind Abbey House in Abingdon yielded fourteen skeletons. It seemed to follow a row of shallow graves only 3ft deep, 50 yards or so from site of the abbey itself. The skeletons must have been at least sixteenth century in origin, for this lay cemetery, used for between 600 and 700 years, was closed when the abbey was suppressed in 1538. Archaeologists believed that thousands more skeletons could be in the vicinity. (Newsquest Oxfordshire)

Plaque to John Aubrey. The discrepency between the date of birth on the plaque (1625) and the one generally accepted (1626) is due to the use of the old style calender in the first instance, when the year began on 25 March. As Aubrey was born on 12 March, it was technically still 1625! (Newsquest Oxfordshire)

In the churchyard of St Lawrence, Caversfield, a gracious and kindly thought which bridges the centuries led to the erection of this simple cross. The previously unmarked grave is that of warriors killed in a battle which took place some 1,700 years ago. (Newsquest Oxfordshire)

About fifteen 'Cloister Skeletons' were discovered in Oxford at Christ Church in 1985; these included a baby and a 7-year-old. The graves were shallow, only about 2ft below the surface, some stone-lined and others on a bed of charcoal, a standard Saxon method. These were followed in 2006 by seven more skeletons, two adults and five children, believed to be from the fourteenth or fifteenth century, unearthed in Tom Quad at Christ Church. Tony Morris, Clerk of Works at the college, called in archaeologists while routine gas and electrical works were being carried out. It was thought that Tom Quad had been built over the graveyard of the Augustinian Priory of St Frideswide which had previously been on the site.

The remains were sent to the archaeologists' office so that their age, sex and cause of death could be established. The archaeologists believed that these skeletons were only a fragment of the total number buried within the Christ Church site but because it is listed disturbance has to be kept to a minimum.

A great number of unmarked graves were those of paupers, some of them members of families who could not afford to pay for what was considered a decent funeral, others whose identity was unknown even at the time of death. The whereabouts of other graves have simply been forgotten over the years. One of these is that of antiquarian and biographer John Aubrey (1626-1697), who wrote in his *Lives*: 'How these curiosities would be quite forgot, did not such idle fellows as I am put them down.' In addition to writing biographies of the notables of his own age such as Walter Raleigh and Francis Bacon, Aubrey wrote a biography of Shakespeare and was the first person to state that Stonehenge was a Druid temple. His *Lives* was published as *Brief Lives* in 1898.

Aubrey studied law at Oxford but did not take a degree or practise as a lawyer. After being made bankrupt in 1670 by a series of lawsuits following his father's death in 1652, he became dependent on patrons, including the antiquary Elias Ashmole and the philosopher Thomas Hobbes. John Aubrey lies in an unmarked grave somewhere in St Mary Magdalen Church in Oxford.

Inside the Church

Not surprisingly, the more important members of the community were usually buried inside the church building and so their tombs and monuments are generally in better condition than those which have had to withstand conditions in the churchyard, although this did not protect them from wear and tear and in some cases actual vandalism. In the case of stone effigies it is not unusual to find missing or replaced noses and hands while some monumental brasses have been stolen for the value of their metal content. Some late-medieval brasses were deliberately defaced by members of the family who feared reprisals about so-called 'popish' features.

Over the centuries, tombs and monuments from all periods have been moved from their original sites to more convenient places during extension and repairs of the church or chapel in which they lie. A drastic example of this is the case of Geoffrey Barbour, a Welsh merchant who had made his money in Bristol. He is known to have been in Abingdon by 1375 when there are records of his renting a shop from the abbey. According to the terms of his will made in 1392, as part of a series of charitable bequests, money went to the upkeep of the town's bridges. Barbour died in 1417 and was buried in the abbey church. When it was demolished after the dissolution of the abbey in 1538, his bones and monumental brass were moved to St Helen's, where the brass is still to be found in the St Katharine aisle.

The earliest form of memorial was a plain slab, often with an incised cross, which formed the lid of the coffin. The names of the deceased are usually missing from monuments until the later Middle Ages, the identification being by heraldic shields which would have been easier to interpret than lettering for the largely illiterate parishioners. After the Dissolution many graves were plundered and stone coffin lids removed to be sold as paving stones.

An early inscription in rather crude lettering can be found in Christ Church Cathedral. This was originally at Osney Abbey and is on the gravestone of Ela, Countess of Warwick, who died in 1297.

Also in the cathedral is the shrine of St Frideswide (*c.* 680–727), a Saxon princess who founded a priory on the site. Her church was burnt down, along with members of Oxford's Danish community who had sought refuge inside it, in 1002. It was reconstructed as a monastery church between *c.* 1150 and 1210 as an Augustinian monastery, which lasted until 1524 when it was suppressed, although the church itself survived to later become both the chapel of the college of Christ Church and the cathedral of the newly-created diocese of Oxford.

Alabaster was not used for monuments until the beginning of the fourteenth century; the earliest in the county is a knight of about 1400 in Dorchester Abbey.

Monumental brasses are incised likenesses which may be found on tomb-chests or set into floors. A great number of these have been repositioned on walls to preserve them and others are now protected by carpets. Some brasses are contemporary with the date of death of the person depicted and maybe a portrait, but others were obviously executed at a later date, probably by descendants of the deceased. Brasses are very important to historians of costume and armour for most of them were done in great detail, down to hairstyles and footwear. The earliest English brasses date from the thirteenth century and although Oxfordshire does not have any of the oldest specimens, it does have some excellent ones. The county ranks fifth in the number of brasses it contains, after Kent, Norfolk, Essex and Suffolk. In Oxfordshire there are numerous examples of fourteenth-century knights in armour, the earlier ones wearing chain-mail, then after the middle of the century, plate armour.

In St Andrew's Church at Chinnor is one of the largest collections of brasses in England; the majority are fourteenth-century knights, priests and civilians.

A late-medieval type of monument is the tomb-chest, which was common until the middle of the sixteenth century and enjoyed a revival in Victorian times.

During the later Middle Ages people became obsessed with the idea of mortality and the corruption of the flesh. Effigies, brasses, paintings and epitaphs contain references to the fact that the dead were once warm flesh and blood and that all too soon the reader would be in a similar condition. A Tudor alternative was to show the deceased wearing shrouds, examples of which can be found at Appleton, Childrey, Longworth, Corpus Christi and New Colleges, Shipton-under-Wychwood, while at Oddington, Ralph Hamsterley is shown as a skeleton in his shroud. The brass of William Gibson and his wife of Watlington has the couple shown in their shrouds with the ends tied above their heads and the date 1501. This brass was stolen in the nineteenth century and ended up in a private collection of such items. When it was put on display at Cambridge, however, it was recognized and eventually returned to its original home.

St Frideswide's shrine, originally constructed in 1289, was destroyed at the Reformation when the saint's bones were removed and subsequently mislaid. Some time later, Katherine Martyr, wife of one of the cathedral canons, was buried near the site. At the Counter-Reformation an enquiry decided that Protestant Katherine had been buried too close to the saint, so her remains were taken off to a dung-heap. When Elizabeth I restored Protestantism to England, a respectable reburial was ordered for Katherine, and around the same time, a package of bones wrapped in silk was discovered in the cathedral. These were accepted as those of St Frideswide, and both ladies were re-interred in a shared grave on 11 January 1562. Fragments of the original shrine were incorporated into one which was rebuilt in 1889 and restored in 2002.

When this tomb in the parish church of St Peter in the East was opened in 1968 and the coffin lid removed, the remains of the unknown occupant could be seen inside the burial sacking. (Newsquest Oxfordshire)

This life-sized effigy of a bishop in All Saints' Church, Didcot, is thought to be Ralph de Dudcote who died in 1293. (Newsquest Oxfordshire)

Opposite: The Lady Chapel at Dorchester Abbey has a rare figure of a crusader, Sir John Holcombe, who was killed in 1280 whilst taking part in the Second Crusade. He lies frozen in stone in the act of drawing his sword. This 'action statue' is very different from the usual effigies, which lie in repose. (Newsquest Oxfordshire)

In the Golafre Chapel at Fyfield church is the impressive tomb of Sir John Golafre, a favourite of Henry VI who knighted him. Golafre lived at the manor house next to the church and was an influential member of Abingdon's Fraternity of the Holy Cross. He died in 1442 and the conventional effigy on the top of the tomb shows him as a knight in full armour, but underneath is a cadaver complete with the round mop of closely trimmed hair which fifteenth-century knights wore to protect their scalps from helmets. This statue must have given generations of children nightmares.

The Church of St Peter and St Paul at Wantage has a dual dedication owing to the fact that there were once two churches in this churchyard, the other having been demolished in the mid-nineteenth century. Inside the surviving building is a 5ft-tall brass to Ivo Fitzwarren (d. 1412) whom some people suppose to have been the father of Alice, who appears in pantomime as the sweetheart and future wife of Dick Whittington.

Childrey, in the Vale of White Horse, has a portrait gallery of brasses. These are relatively late examples which date mainly from the mid-fifteenth and early-sixteenth centuries. Among them are William Fettiplace who died in 1516 and his wife, who are shown kneeling in shrouds. Dorchester Abbey has the brass of Abbot Beauforest, who bought the dissolved abbey church in 1536 for £140 for use of the people of the town as a parish church, so saving it from destruction.

In Christ Church Cathedral is the Purbeck marble tomb of Bishop Robert King, who survived the dissolution of Osney Abbey to become the first bishop of Oxford.

Pupils at Chinnor Church of England School recording their heritage by preparing an exhibition, part of which was a display of brass rubbings from St Andrew's Church. The knight in this rubbing is Reginald de Malyns, who died around 1385, and is portrayed with his two wives. (Newsquest Oxfordshire)

Some tomb-chests, like this one to Sir John Clerke at Thame, had brasses and canopies. Sir John, who died in 1539, is shown with bobbed hair and wearing armour, gilded spurs and a cloak embroidered with swans. In 1513 he took part in the Battle of the Spurs where he took prisoner a French duke whose helm, decorated with ram's horns, hangs above the tomb. (Newsquest Oxfordshire)

Thomas, the son of Geoffrey Chaucer, died in 1434 and is buried with his wife, Matilda Burghersh, in the parish church at Ewelme. On their tomb are brass figures showing Thomas in plate armour with the Chaucer unicorn at his feet, while Matilda's rest on a lion with a forked tail. Thomas, who was Member of Parliament for Oxfordshire and four times Speaker of the House of Commons, acquired the manor of Ewelme when he married Matilda. The heraldic shields on the side of the tomb show Thomas's descent and family connections. (Newsquest Oxfordshire)

King died in 1557 and had a brass effigy, which has now disappeared; above the tomb, however, is a memorial window showing him in his bishop's regalia, looking saturnine and handsome, standing in front of Osney Abbey. This picture of the abbey is important as it shows the building as it was before it was dismantled and much of the fabric brought into Oxford to be used in what is now Christ Church.

The parish church of St Peter in the East (now the library of St Edmund Hall) has a brass commemorating Mrs Elizabeth Parret (*née* Love) of Ayno, Northamptonshire who was born around 1527. She died in childbirth on Christmas Eve, 1572, and was buried at St Peter's the following day. In the same church is a brass to Simon Parret (d. 1584) which reads:

> Here resteth the bodies of Simon Parret Gentilman : master of arte: late fellowe of Magdalen Colledge and twice procter of the Universitie of Oxford : and Eliza: beth his wife, daughter of Edward Love of Aenohe in the Countie of North hampton Esquier : which Simon departed this worlde the 24: day of Septebr in the yeare of our lorde God MCCCCC 84 and in the yere of his age 71: and Elizabeth departed in childbed the xxiiii day of December in the yere of oure lorde God MCCCCC lxxii : and in the yere of her age xlv.

As a result, Elizabeth Parret is commemorated on two separate brasses, her own and her husband's.

Not all brasses are centuries old. Major restoration to the Church of St Bartholomew at Yarnton was carried out and financed by William Fletcher, an Oxford draper, in 1793. Fletcher, who died in 1826 and is described as 'Alderman of

Opposite from top:
At Broughton, in the church which is situated across the moat from the castle, the very colourful early fourteenth-century effigy of John de Broughton wears a suit of chain-mail and has with him his sword and shield. His legs are crossed, he has a lion at his feet and his pillow is supported by two angels. In the Oxfordshire volume of Pevsner's *The Buildings of England* series he states that both the effigy and the elaborate recess in which it lies were 'both violently coloured in 1846.' This was not merely another example of the Victorian desire to improve on the work of earlier generations, for much medieval work would have been highly coloured, although in the vast majority of cases the most evidence that remains are traces of paint. This effigy is unusual in that it is still in its original place.

Pevsner makes an interesting comment about two more Broughton effigies, the knight and lady in the chancel. The knight is believed to be Sir Thomas Wykeham who died in 1470, and has 'a vigorously carved head with forceful features' but his companion is dressed in a style from the earlier part of the fifteenth century, and her effigy 'stylized and impersonal'.

This fourteenth-century tomb-chest at Cogges, which has a female effigy with lions at her feet, angels supporting the pillow and symbols of the Evangelists, was intended for Isabelle de Grey but it is by no means certain that she does in fact occupy it, and the shields on the side of the tomb, which remain blank, offer no proof. (Newsquest Oxfordshire)

John de Broughton
lder of the Church
1306

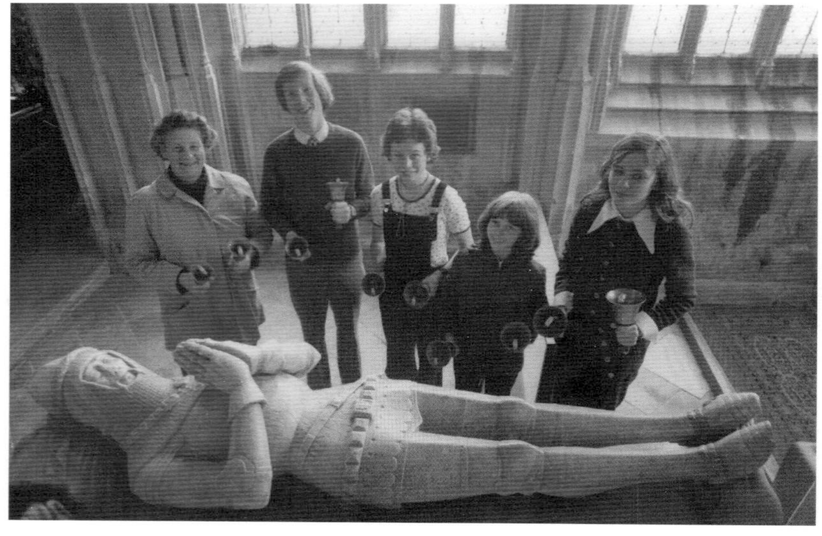

the City of Oxford, philotheus and philanthropos of Oxford', lies here in a medieval stone coffin which came from the Godstow nunnery, in a table-tomb which he designed himself. Fletcher's portrait brass, which portrays him in his alderman's robes, is copied from that of Richard Atkinson (d. 1674) in the Church of St Peter in the East, Oxford. The epitaph was written by William Fletcher himself.

There are a small number of fine brasses which date from Victorian times and are influenced by the revival of interest in all things medieval. These commemorate high-ranking churchmen such as canons and bishops and show an immense amount of detail. Examples of Victorian brasses can be found in the cathedral, notably that of Frederick Barnes (d. 1859) in the cathedral's lady chapel.

A feature of memorials of notable people is the use of statuary in which the deceased are shown as figures reclining on tombs or on wall monuments, frequently kneeling in family groups with large numbers of children, the sons behind their father, and the daughters behind their mother. Earlier effigies are probably not portraits but later ones are much more realistic and in some cases family resemblances are quite marked.

The church of the Holy Rood at Sparsholt has three larger-than-life wooden figures, those of Sir Robert Archard, who died in 1353, and his two wives. They are made of hollow oak and were once painted and gilded. By contrast, another memorial at Sparsholt is to a dwarf of the Fettiplace family.

According to the prevailing fashion, some effigies portray the deceased as a decomposing corpse, complete with worms and sometimes even with a scar where the internal organs had been removed prior to the time when embalming became fashionable.

Opposite from top:

The present church of St Mary at Ewelme was started about 1430, replacing an earlier one dedicated to All Saints. It was completed mid-century and has brick battlements and squared stones and flints, which are unusual in Oxfordshire and gives it the appearance of an East Anglia church. Duchess Alice's tomb, which dates from about 1475, shows her wearing a coronet. On her left arm is the Garter, which is so unusual for a woman that when Queen Victoria needed to know how to wear it correctly a study was made of the Duchess's effigy. She lies in all her glory on the top of the stone chest, but another statue below shows her as a cadaver. (Newsquest Oxfordshire)

In the Wilcote Chapel at North Leigh, Sir William Wilcote, who died in 1410, lies in a magnificent suit of armour on an alabaster tomb. He was Member of Parliament for Oxfordshire from 1386 to 1396 and Sheriff of Oxfordshire and Berkshire in 1392. His wife Elizabeth, who married Sir John Blackett after Wilcote's death, has a jewelled headband and hairnet and both wear the Lancastrian SS collar, which is unusual for a woman. The parents of William Lenthall, Speaker of the House of Commons, are also buried at North Leigh. The church is the proud possessor of a rare collection of coffin plates. (Newsquest Oxfordshire)

The Lovell family built the imposing Minster Lovell Hall that now lies in ruins on the banks of the Windrush nearby. An earlier member of the family, Francis, Baron Lovell, appears in Shakespeare and, along with associates named Catesby and Ratcliffe, was a favourite of Richard III. Their names gave rise to the rhyme,

The Cat, the Rat, and Lovell, the dog
Rule all England under a Hog.

Lovell was known as 'the King's Spaniel' and the 'hog' is a reference to the white boar, which was part of Richard III's coat-of-arms. Lovell was given the task of preventing Henry Tudor from landing in England in order to take the crown from Richard, but Tudor managed to elude him and, after winning the Battle of Bosworth Field in 1485, eventually became Henry VII.

Lovell did not learn his lesson but went on to become involved in the plot to replace Henry with a pretender named Lambert Simnel. In 1487, he fought for Simnel at the Battle of Stoke, after which his future remains a mystery. He was last seen crossing the river on his horse and rumour said that he made his way back to Minster Lovell where, in the safety of his ancestral home, he took refuge in a secret room. Only a servant knew his whereabouts and, when this man died, Lovell was left locked in the room where he starved to death. There may be some truth in this story for when repairs were being carried out in 1708, a secret room was discovered. Inside was a skeleton seated at a table on which was a book. Nearby was the skeleton of a dog.

On the wall of the south transept of Adderbury church is a painted wooden panel with effigies of Thomas and Mary More (1586) who are kneeling by a tomb and inform the reader that:

We have been flesh and now we are but bones,
And lie for other flesh to take their view:
Our sides were never brass, our strength not stones,
We could not choose but bid the world adieu.
So far is aught from lasting aye
That tombs shall have their dying day.

Opposite: The Harcourt family, which traced its ancestry back to Bernard the Dane, who lived in the ninth century, occupy some of the most notable tombs in Oxfordshire. These range in date from medieval to Victorian times and are to be found in Stanton Harcourt church. The most notable, Robert Harcourt, also fought at Bosworth Field but on the opposite side from Francis Lovell as he was standard-bearer to Henry VII. Harcourt lies on a canopied tomb decorated with monks, angels and the Lancastrian red rose. Over the tomb are a helm and a fragment of the flag believed to have been carried by Harcourt on the day that the last of the Plantagenet kings was killed and the Tudor dynasty began. (Newsquest Oxfordshire)

Above: This photograph, taken in the church of St Kenelm, Minster Lovell, shows the tomb and effigy of William, 7th Baron Lovell, who died in 1455.

At Bampton George Thomson, who died in 1603, is shown bearded and wearing ruffs at his neck and wrists, lying on a large tomb with a canopy. His epitaph reads:

> Heaven hath my soul in happiest joy and bliss:
> Earth hath my earth, where body tombèd is.
> Poor have my store, for ever to their use:
> Friends have my name, to keep without abuse.
> Heaven, earth, poor, friends, of me have had their part,
> And this in life was chiefest joy of heart.

A strange form of haunting took place on No. 6 staircase at Exeter College on 13 October 1916. The story was reported in the *Oxford Mail* of 2 November 1966, half a century after it happened.

Opposite and right: The Fettiplace memorials in Swinbrook church in the Windrush Valley are both startling and unique. Almost one entire wall of the chancel is occupied by two sets of monuments erected in 1613 and 1686, each adorned with three armoured effigies lying propped up on an elbow, stacked one above the other as if on shelves. The figures, which range in date from Anthony (1510) to Edmund (1686), are uncannily alike, and are surrounded by later members of the same family. Despite this impressive display of testosterone, the direct male Fettiplace line ran out in 1743. (Newsquest Oxfordshire)

As an undergraduate, the composer Thomas Wood had rooms at the top of the staircase, five flights up. Wood was just leaving for a coffee party in a friend's rooms and had already turned out the light before closing the door when he stopped abruptly in his tracks, shocked rigid by what he saw in the doorway:

> A man was standing right up against me with the narrow band of light under Sharp's door shining through his body, and he had no head. Words won't come fast enough, buff coat; yellow slashings; black gown; one hand up as though he were going to knock; the bright pinpoint of Sharp's keyhole where his heart should be, and where his face should be . . . nothing. He stood still while I could have counted one, two, three, four, and my hair bristled. Then he went – puff – out like a candle.

This ostentatious tomb which obstructs the chancel in St Mary's Church, Thame, is that of Lord Williams of Thame and his wife. It was the first Oxfordshire tomb to include Renaissance embellishment, which broke away from formal designs in favour of greater realism. As Sir John Williams, he acquired the manors of Thame from the Crown after the Reformation. He lived nearby at Rycote House, where he was gaoler to the Princess Elizabeth before she became queen. At the suppression of Thame Abbey he bought the buildings and surrounding parkland. He died aged 59 in 1559 and left money to endow a grammar school and almshouses in Church Road. The inmates of the almshouses, five men and a solitary woman, were given a black woollen gown every year on All Souls Day and every fourth Christmas a red gown for Sunday best. As a demonstration of their gratitude they were required, health permitting, to attend morning and evening church services daily, and on Sundays and holy days to sit around their benefactor's tomb. Both almshouses and grammar school still exist although nowadays neither serves its original purpose. (Newsquest Oxfordshire)

Of course there was a search, but nothing suspicious was discovered. Wood came in for a good deal of teasing for having imagined such a visitor while still sober, even though it had happened at Hallowe'en.

The following day, however, Wood's tutor told him about something that had happened the previous day, in fact the same morning that his mysterious visitor had called. Work had begun on clearing out lumber from underneath No. 6 staircase and by the evening most of it had been cleared. Among the items which had come to light was a statue which appeared to be of a man in seventeenth-century dress, and, although it was rather battered, still of interest. The tutor suggested that Wood go and see for himself, so down he went to the basement, where he found a little figure of a man kneeling at prayer.

Wood recalled that,

> He was wearing his gown and a tunic that had slashed sleeves edged with lace around the wrists. Faint traces of colour were left: brown. He had no head. My hair bristled for the second time. I had seen the original of this battered piece of marble. He came to knock at my door last night.

The monument was identified as belonging to John Crocker, a gentleman-commoner from Devon, who had died on 29 April 1629. It had been stored away out of sight under No. 6 staircase since the 1850s, when the seventeenth-century chapel had been demolished to make way for the present one. Even though a name had been attached to the figure, the reason why John Crocker waited until 1916 and then chose Thomas Wood in his eyrie five flights up as his target has never been explained.

Whatever the reason, John Crocker was immediately locked away behind the chapel doors in case he tries to scare future Hallowe'en revellers.

The painted statue discovered at Exeter College. (Newsquest Oxfordshire)

Inside the church at Burford is the alabaster tomb of Sir Lawrence Tanfield, Chief Baron of the Exchequer to Queen Elizabeth I. Sir Lawrence wears a ruff and scarlet-lined cloak. His entry in the parish burial register for reads:

> Sir Laurence [*sic*] Tanfield, Knighte, Lorde Chfe Baron of his Mates. Courte of Exchequer was buried the first of May at 12 of the clocke in the night, he departinge this life about two of the clocke in the morning upon Satterdie the laste of April 1625.

Next to him lies Lady Tanfield, dressed in black and gold. Her burial entry refers to:

> Tanfield, Elizabeth Dame Tanfield, wife unto Sr Lawrence [*sic*] Tanfield Knighte, Lord Chiefe Baron of his Maties. Court of Exchequere, who died the 21st daie of Julie.

Near them is their daughter Elizabeth, wife of 1st Viscount Falkland, and the diminutive effigy of their grandson, Lucius Cary, also forms part of the tomb. Lady Tanfield wrote of him,

> In Bliss is Hee whom I loved best,
> Thrise happie Shee with him to rest.

The family is buried in the church in their home village of Great Tew. On the lower part of the Tanfield tomb is a skeleton lying on a mattress.

The Tanfields were so heartily loathed in Burford and so evil was their reputation that Lady Tanfield is said to haunt the town, flying over the rooftops in a blazing coach. Another version of the story has Tanfield himself driving a phantom team over the Burford skyline. Eventually the townspeople engaged a local clergyman to perform an exorcism. Lady Tanfield's spirit was trapped in a glass bottle which was sealed and thrown into the Windrush, near the bridge. If the cork ever dried out, so says a local rumour, her spirit may escape, and so to prevent this happening Burford residents would top up the river with buckets of water.

In Spelsbury church is the tomb of Sir Henry Lee, the ancestor of the American general, Robert E. Lee. Sir Henry died in 1631 and years later, in 1645, George Pickering, the Lees' servant for more than thirty years, was buried nearby. Pickering is described as 'creeping neere their tombes adored side, to show his body, not his duty dyde.'

Of course not all monuments have effigies. At Burford the 1569 monument to Edmund Harman and his wife includes no effigy of the couple themselves but does have rows of 'cheerful children tightly packed' on the front of it. Also according to Pevsner, the inscription has 'Red Indians disporting themselves on it.' Harman was barber to Henry VIII and was rewarded with gifts of land and property for his

The Tanfield memorial, Burford.

services, including the Hospital of St John the Evangelist at Burford, along with other places along the Oxfordshire-Gloucestershire border. What connection these Native Americans have with Burford is still a mystery.

Christ Church Cathedral contains many monuments from the 1640s, when the Court was at Oxford. In the south transept are memorials to several cavaliers, three of whom were Charles I's Stuart cousins.

Under the years 1643-4 the cathedral's burial register lists the Sergeant of the Counting House; the Clerk Comptroller; the Yeoman of the Wardrobe; two Governors of the city of Oxford; two Garter Heralds; the Comptroller of the King's House; several Major Generals and Lieutenant Colonels; the Lord Chief Justice of the Common Pleas and Privy Councillor; the Captain of Horse, and the Keeper of the Great Seal of England.

Twenty years later the cathedral saw the funeral of the Earl of Newport, of which Anthony Wood writes:

> Mountjoy Blount, gentleman of the bedchamber to his majestie, died of a violent fit of the stone in the larg freestone house in Slaying Lane [Brewer Street] in St Aldate's parish, M. 12 feb; and was buried in the south isle joining to Ch Church choire neare to the grave of the lord Grandison.

Monument to Edmund Harman. (Newsquest Oxfordshire)

This photograph, taken in May 1975, shows expert restoration being carried out on the memorial of Francesca Thornehill, who died in 1640. Under the floor of the chapel, which is in the Church of St Peter and Paul at Aston Rowant, are several coffins containing members of the family. (Newsquest Oxfordshire)

The seventeenth century brought a new fashion in which the deceased were portrayed kneeling at prayer rather than just lying on the tomb. These figures were of marble which was highly painted and gilded. Thirty years later, however, tastes changed yet again in favour of more restrained memorials.

The story of Anthony Wood (or à Wood, as he later styled himself), begins with his birth in 1632 at Postmasters Hall, a Merton property in Merton Street, and ends with his death in the same house in 1695. His autobiography covers the reigns of Charles I and the Commonwealth and those of Charles II, James II, and William and Mary.

Wood's first work, *History and Antiquities of Oxford*, met with a good reception when it came out in 1674. However, his *Athenae Oxonienses*, the first volume of which appeared in 1691, was an account of the City and University of Oxford and included uncomplimentary descriptions of several leading members, which provoked an outburst of criticism and protest. The second volume, which appeared the following year, was publicly burnt and its author expelled from membership of the University.

Wood's entries on life in Oxford during the Civil War are very enlightening. The activities of the Court of Charles I and Henrietta Maria, which was at Oxford from 1642 to 1646, come under particular criticism, a very different picture from that created later by romantic novelists.

According to Wood the behaviour of the Court of Charles II, which moved to Oxford during outbreaks of plague in London in the 1660s, was even less praiseworthy. The courtiers might have been 'neat and gay in their apparell, but they were very nasty and beastly, leaving at their departure their excrements in every corner, in chimneys, studies, colehouses, cellars. Rude, rough, whoremongers; vaine, empty, carelesse.'

Wood suffered from the painful suppression of urine, a condition which was eventually to kill him. In 1695, his doctor's way of telling Wood that he could do nothing for him was to say that if he could not make water he must make earth, and indeed he was dead in under a week. He was buried in the ante-chapel of Merton College chapel, in a grave which he had selected (he is also reported to have also dug the grave himself), five years before he occupied it.

On the wall of the nave of West Hanney church is a memorial to Elizabeth Bowls, who, we read, died 1718 aged 124 but it is unclear whether the lady was buried inside the church or in the churchyard.

The eighteenth century was a time of excess in monuments as in other things and there are some grand examples complete with life-size figures in classical dress, urns and mourning ladies. Some of these take up an entire chapel wall from floor to ceiling. Among the most startling is one at Steeple Aston made by Scheemakers in 1730 for Sir Francis and Lady Page. Pevsner calls Judge Page a 'Gilbert and

Above, left: A feature of memorials of the 1660s and '70s was the vogue for well-executed stonewall tablets, one of which is the Blake memorial at Cogges which has busts of William, who died in 1695, Sarah in 1701, and Francis in 1681. They are listed in the burial register as being of Highgate in the County of Middlesex. This William Blake gave Witney its Butter Cross in order to provide protection from the weather for the women who sold butter and their produce. He also founded the school which bears his name. The memorial tablet mentions William himself, his son Francis and his daughter-in-law Sarah, all of whom are buried in the family vault at Cogges. (Newsquest Oxfordshire)

Above, right: At Spelsbury, the 3rd Earl of Lichfield who died in 1772, has grey and gold monument with coffin, snake and cherub busily tying inscriptions to an oak tree.

Sullivan figure' and his wife 'dumpy'. When he noticed that his wife's statue wore no wedding ring Page refused to pay Scheemakers for his work but eventually £10 was deducted from the bill as compensation.

Although hundreds of people are buried inside church or chapel buildings, many of them have no surviving memorial of any kind, and it is impossible to know if any ever existed.

The inevitable route to the grave is described by Anthony Wood on several occasions. On 19 January 1643 his father died,

> ... to the very great grief and reluctancy of his wife and children ... and being a fat and corpulent man, and therefore his body could not keep, he was buried between 8 and 9 of

> the clock and night on the same day in the north part of Merton coll. Outer-chapell or church, neare to the graves of James Wood his younger brother who died in September 1629 and John Wood his son.

And on 22 May 1655, 'Edward Wood died to the great reluctancy of his friends and relations, in his mother's house against Merton Coll.' He died of 'vomiting blood and consumption with it, and made a most religious end.'

On May 24th,

> his body was carried into the common hall of Merton Coll., where the society and such masters of Arts that were pleased to come and pay their last respects to him, had gloves, wine and bisket in abundance, as also had the Doctors, Heades of Houses, and his brother Proctor to which last e Wood had bequeathed money to buy him a mourning gowne. Afterwards his body being carried to Merton coll. Church, there was a sermon preached for that occasion by his aforesaid quondam tutor.

And finally on 28 February 1667 he writes:

> Mary Woode, widow of Thomas Woode, departed this mortal life a 9 of the clock in the morning, about quarter past, having bin a widow 24 years and upwards and in the year of her age 65 and 2 months. She was buried March the 1, F., neare the grave of her husband in Merton College church.

There follows an explicit description of his mother's last illness and various forms of treatment; finally he writes that:

> Apr 2, T, the bones of Thomas Wood, father to A.W. were taken up, and laid close to those of his wife. My father's bones were removed to my mother's grave by old Robert Church, 3/6d.

One unusual burial and the discovery of another took place in Merton College chapel in the second part of the seventeenth century. The burial was that of Edward Price who was, writes Wood, 'the dwarf belonging to Mert. Coll. Buried. He was killed the day before with a fall from one of the warden's coach horses'. His funeral was held on 24 July 1668.

Then, on 4 November 1671, there was considerable excitement when,

> ... the workmen removing the bricks at Mert. Coll. High altar found under the north wall, under Sir Thomas Bodley's monument, a ston coffin: wherein were the bones of a man 6 feet long; his surplice (as it seems) was on him; a long welt downe his brests; and his sandals on his feet; and a chalice, covered, on his breast of pewter. The cover of the coffin lying

The elegant wall monument to Christopher Kempster of Burford, a master-mason who worked with Sir Christopher Wren.

> even with the surface of the bricks was let lower two handsfull. I think they are the bones of Dr Henry de Abenden. The welt or stripe had been painted; the shoes black, flat, round toed. He had neither miter on him or crosier in his hand; and therefore no bishop, as 'twas reported. Some took away his sandals: others some part of the welt.

Registers throughout the country mention the fact that parishioners were buried in wool. This does not mean that the people involved were too poor to afford coffins but refers to the Burial in Wool Act which was passed in 1667 in an attempt to improve the wool trade, which was in the doldrums at that time. The Act 'did enjoyne that they are not to be buried in any shirt, shift, sheet or shroud made or mingled with flax, hemp, silk, hair, gold, or silver or any other than what is made of sheep's wool', the penalty for not complying being £5. An affidavit had to be sworn in front of a magistrate and a certificate issued to confirm that this had been done. The Act was enforced more strictly after 1 August 1678.

In the case of richer people, or those with social aspirations, shrouds were made of linen or more expensive material and this fact, together with the fine paid, may be entered into the burial register. The Burial in Wool Act remained in force until 1814, by which date it had long been ignored. Some of the certificates themselves survive in archives and county record offices among parish records. Those of St Peter ad Vincula, South Newington, which have been deposited in the Oxfordshire County Record Office, include a most unusual collection of burial in wool certificates, some with hearses, skeletons and other symbols of mortality.

Although the vast majority of the population went to their graves in one piece, the practice of removing the heart and, less frequently, the viscera of the deceased before burial was not uncommon among royalty and members of the aristocracy, probably the most famous instance being the heart of Robert the Bruce. An example of a heart burial is found at Adwell where a miniature knight has been holding a heart since about 1300.

Some of the county's churches have entries in the parish registers for the burial of urns containing hearts and other internal organs. The Woodstock register reads that on 30 September 1670, 'The bowels of Lord Lovlass [Lovelace] were buried in Woodstock Church' and a later entry from 1702 is 'The Bowels of Henry Meux of Pagham in the Isle of Wight interred.' Mr Meux was a former curate and the rest of the reverend gentleman would have returned home.

In the Churchyard

Although the last resting-places of the more influential members of society are to be found inside the church, nearly all parish churchyards can offer a wealth of interest and information.

However, obtaining and using a plot of land suitable for use as a burial ground has not always been as straightforward as it might seem. In the Middle Ages those of some religious foundations and minsters claimed exclusivity, for instance the only place of burial for Abingdon and the surrounding villages was the lay cemetery of the abbey. At this time the parish church, St Helen's, did not have its own cemetery as the abbey had the monopoly on burials. The citizens sought approval for a piece of land adjoining the church being used for the interment of their own dead, which infuriated the abbot because the burial fees, which he considered should go to the abbey, were being paid to the incumbent of St Helen's. In 1392 two corpses from Shippon were actually hijacked and the cortège forced into the abbey cemetery. Eventually, in 1396 the Pope decided in favour of the abbot and against the vicar and parishioners. A long-lasting difficulty at St Helen's, when people forgot to fasten the gates securely, was the pigs, which roamed around the churchyard and dug up the corpses. Another problem was the monks' tendency to take away the tombstones and either using or selling them. Burial was not sanctioned in St Helen's churchyard until after the abbey was dissolved. The Abingdon case was exceptional and on the whole the rest of the county's churchyards have had a long and peaceful history.

The Burford burial registers record that on 30 January 1626, Innocent Grinnowaie was interred in the churchyard, 'being 105 yeares ould'. It is unlikely that Mr Grinnowaie's grave was ever marked by a stone for, had it survived, it would certainly have become an attraction for visitors.

The grave of John Young in St Andrew's churchyard, Old Headington.

Some surviving gravestones do record extraordinarily long lives, most of which we are unable to either confirm or deny. One of the best known of these is to be found in St Andrew's churchyard, Old Headington, where the renovated stone of John Young is to be found near the south-west entrance. We read that John died in 1688 at the age of 100, which means that he was born in the year of the Armada and lived until the Glorious Revolution. His inscription reads:

> Here Lyeth John
> Who to ye King did belong
> He liv'd to be old
> And yet dyed young

A grave at Sutton Courtenay commemorates someone who may have lived even longer than John Young. This is Mrs Martha Pye, who died in 1822, when, says the burial register, she was 'said to be 117 years old'.

Also at Sutton Courtenay is a more verifiable claim to longevity, that of John Faulkener who died in 1933 when he was nearly 105. Apart from his age, Faulkener may claim to be the country's oldest jockey. He rode his first winner when he was only eight and his last, at Abingdon Races, when he was 74.

Some graves are notable for their construction and inscriptions rather than their occupants. Other Oxfordshire graves are those of people who are not household names but who for various reasons are nevertheless well known locally.

In 1658 a man with a world-famous name was buried at Kirtlington. Called Christopher Wren, he was the father of the great architect Sir Christopher Wren, who is, of course, buried in London in St Paul's Cathedral. The family's connections with Oxfordshire go back to Christopher Wren senior's time, when he came up to Oxford to study at St John's College. After graduating he entered the Church and in 1620 was appointed rector of the Wiltshire parishes of Fonthill (where he married the squire's daughter and heiress, Mary Cox) and three years later of East Knoyle. All the couple's children were born at East Knoyle, including Christopher in 1632. In 1634 Wren became Dean of Windsor in place of his brother Matthew, who had been made Bishop of Hereford. Christopher Wren senior returned to Oxfordshire to spend his last years at Kirtlington, a St John's College living.

Another 'same name' burial took place at the tiny church of St Lawrence, North Hinksey, in 1922. The person in question was Sir Walter Raleigh, whose gravestone can be seen in the churchyard there. He was born in London in 1861 and went first to the City of London School and Edinburgh Academy, then on to University College London, and King's College, Cambridge. He held the posts of Professor of English Literature at the Mohammedan Anglo-Oriental College in Aligarh, Professor of Modern Literature at University College Liverpool, Regius Professor of English Language and Literature at Glasgow University, and Professor of English Literature at the University of Oxford University, where he became a Fellow of Merton College. Professor Raleigh was knighted in 1911. The family lived at Harcourt Hill from 1909 to 1922 and nearby Raleigh Park is named after him. Professor Sir Walter Raleigh died from typhoid which he had contracted in the Middle East.

A curious literary connection is associated with the churchyard at Banbury. Ancient tombs and gravestones have received rough treatment over the years but one of them was once clear enough for the name on it to appeal to Jonathan Swift, who included it in his novel *Gulliver's Travels*, published in 1726. The Gulliver family lived in Banbury for generations and it is the inscription to one of its members, Lemuel, which caught Swift's eye.

In the churchyard at Sandford St Martin is a curious construction described in the *Victoria County History of Oxfordshire* as 'the humpbacked tomb of the earl and countess of Deloraine.' The earl, Henry Scott, was the son of James, Duke of

EHA 757

Monmouth, who was himself the illegitimate son of Charles II and Lucy Walter but was executed for treason by his uncle, James II, when he led an uprising against him.

The brick tomb, which houses the earl, who died in 1730, and his wife Anne, who died ten years earlier, is covered with turf and was originally open at both ends. It was later closed in as it attracted the attentions of local youths.

In 1789 the unusually-named Gravelline Boswell was buried in the churchyard at Stanford in the Vale and in 1824 Charles Hatt Whitfield, also of Stanford, died on 8 December aged 29. His inscription reads:

Stop!
For you like I are bound to die
Consider this O man.

A curiosity of the churchyard of St Peter in the East, which has been deconsecrated and converted into the library of St Edmund Hall, is the gravestone of Sarah Hounslow, who, one reads, died on 31 February 1833. In September 1985 the *Oxford Star* carried a curious account of the Hounslow family of which it states, this 'unusual memorial appears to be the only remaining record' and asks anyone with more information to contact the newspaper. However, a search of St Peter in the East burial register shows that there are several Hounslow entries, including one which records that Sarah, of the High Street, was buried on 27 February 1835, aged 38.

There is plenty of information about Richard Claridge of Spelsbury, who dropped dead at the age of 45 and on whose grave was inscribed:

A sudden call, I in a moment fell,
I had no time to bid my friends farewell,
So you, my neighbours, a warning take,
And love my children for my sake.

Opposite from top:
Banbury town cemetery. In 1971 the Town Clerk of Banbury received a candle and box of matches through the post. This unusual gift was believed to have been sent by a clergyman as a reminder that the lighting in the chapel was inadequate. The candle and matches were forwarded to the Superintendent of the town's parks and cemeteries to be brought up for discussion. The Town Clerk stated that the installation of electricity in the chapel had been rejected because the building was seldom used for services. (Newsquest Oxfordshire)

An unusual journey to the grave took place in Banbury in January 1974 when a Midland Red bus was used as a hearse for the funeral of bus driver Dennis Macarthy. The bus had a wreath attached to its radiator and the pall-bearers were fellow bus drivers dressed in their uniforms. (Newsquest Oxfordshire)

The Deloraine hump-back tomb at Sandford St Martin.

Sarah Hounslow. (Newsquest Oxfordshire)

The first shot fired at the Battle of Waterloo in 1815 is said to have been fired by an Oxfordshire man, Private William Dyke of the 1st Foot (later Grenadier) Guards, although there is no documentary evidence to either confirm or deny this story. At any rate, Dyke returned safely home to England, achieved the rank of sergeant and ended his days in 1866 aged 71 as a Chelsea Out-Pensioner at Burcot. He is commemorated by this small cross near the south wall of the church.

According to Elsie Corbett's book *Spelsbury*, which was published in 1962, this was not the last which was seen of Mr Claridge. His ghost, which appeared in the mid-1830s at nearby Taston, was instantly recognised by the people to whom it manifested itself. Mr Harris of Middle Farm was courting the Widow Claridge of Lower Farm. They were stood by the door talking one evening when the ghost of the lately deceased brushed in between them and made its way into the house. Mr Harris was so unnerved by this obvious objection that he promptly called off the wedding.

In 1846, the villagers of Sandford St Martin put up a memorial to William Williams, who was born in the parish on 16 August 1775 and 'who, while a poor soldier, was presented with a Bible by a bookseller of whom he was about to purchase it and by God's grace and blessing on the use of it, entered in the service of the King of kings and after two years of patient suffering in his bed, fell asleep in Jesus, aged 71.'

Margaret Pattison Thom was born on 20 October 1873 in Matata, New Zealand; her mother was Maori, her father British. Her early years were spent with her Maori family, where she absorbed their language and traditions. She is known by scholars as Makereti, the Maori equivalent of Margaret.

After having a conventional English education, she became a guide showing visitors round the hot geysers near Rororua in New Zealand's North Island and telling them about Maori culture. She changed her name to Maggie Papakur, after one of the geysers, and became something of a local celebrity, appearing in the newspapers and even on postcards.

She joined a group which performed songs and dances for tourists and toured Australia and Britain. While acting as a guide she had met Englishman Richard Staples-Browne and in 1912 came over to England to marry him. They lived at Oddington Grange on the edge of Otmoor and their son, William, went to the Queen's College in 1921 to read anthropology.

New Zealand servicemen recuperating in Oxfordshire were made welcome at Oddington where Maggie later put up a memorial in the church in recognition of the part that Maori soldiers had played in the war.

The Pitt Rivers Museum in Oxford has a unique collection of Maori artefacts obtained from a New Zealand woman who lived in Oddington and was a member of the university. (Newsquest Oxfordshire)

These flowers on a gipsy grave at Radley were photographed in 1979; note the floral caravan at the top left of the picture. (Newsquest Oxfordshire)

When her marriage broke up, she started to study anthropology at the University. In 1927, when she was in her mid-fifties, she became a member of the Society of Oxford Home-Students and began writing a thesis on Maori culture. By this time, though, her health was poor and she was very short of cash. On 16 April 1930, before her thesis was finished, she died of a ruptured aneurysm. Maggie was buried in the churchyard at Oddington and a memorial erected to her in her home town in New Zealand. Initially her grave had only a simple wooden cross but later her countrymen placed a bronze plaque underneath it. The grave is visited from time to time by Maoris, some of whom have come dressed in native costume and performed a Maori lament for Makereti.

An extraordinary form of burial took place at Thame Park. The subject was Sophia Wykeham, Lady Wenman, who at one time was considered to be a prospective wife for the Duke of Clarence. She died at Thame Park in 1870, at the age of 80. It was rumoured that she left instructions that she should be placed in an open coffin in the Wenman crypt and left for a week after her death in case she was not really dead. Obsessive as this may sound, there was a possibility of this really happening in Victorian England. A hole was ordered to be left in a dome in the top of the coffin, which was not to be placed into the ground for fifty years. When Thame Park was sold in the late-twentieth century, the purchasers decided to restore the chapel and the crypt was opened up. When Sophia's coffin was examined it was found that there was in fact no breathing hole; furthermore, in her will there were no directions concerning her burial, and it was concluded that she wanted to be allowed to lie in state for a while. Sophia Wenman was subsequently interred in the burial ground at Thame Park, along with her coronet. The service was attended by some twenty-five guests, one of whom was Bee Gee Robin Gibb, who lives at the Prebendal at Thame.

Oxfordshire has its share of famous people, some of whose graves have become a visitor attraction and in some cases almost a place of pilgrimage. Curiously, the memorials to some of the most interesting people connected with Oxfordshire in modern times are also some of the least impressive and are easily missed.

Sir Winston Leonard Spencer Churchill (1874-1965), the son of Lord Randolph Churchill, was born in Blenheim Palace at Woodstock, the home of his close relative, the Duke of Marlborough. Churchill is buried alongside several other members of his family in the parish churchyard at Bladon, within sight of the palace. Winston Churchill went to Harrow and Sandhurst but not on to university. He spent a short time in the army and became a Conservative Member of Parliament in 1900 and held positions in both Liberal and Conservative governments in the early part of the century. Churchill was Prime Minister from 1940 to 1945 and again from 1951 to 1955, when he resigned office. Nevertheless, he remained an MP until 1964. During the Second World War he had a weekend headquarters in Oxfordshire at Ditchley Park, near Charlbury. In 1947, he was granted the Freedom of the Borough of Woodstock in a ceremony which took place on the steps of the Town Hall.

On his death in 1965, the country went into deep mourning. As the train which brought his body back to Oxfordshire for burial passed through Oxford, Old Tom, the great bell at Christ Church, was tolled. This is an honour normally reserved for a Dean of the college or a reigning monarch. The coffin left the train at Long Hanborough station and the funeral cortège continued on to Bladon by road.

Another Prime Minister, Herbert Henry Asquith (1852-1928), is buried at Sutton Courtenay. After graduating from Balliol College, Asquith entered Parliament in 1886. He served in Campbell-Bannerman's government in 1906 as Home Secretary and Chancellor of the Exchequer, and succeeded him as Prime Minister two years later. The highlight of his premiership, which was marked by industrial problems, demonstrations by the suffragette movement and the ongoing question of Home Rule for Ireland, was the introduction of National Insurance of 1911, which gave insurance cover during periods of illness and unemployment. After heading a coalition government when the First World War broke out, Asquith lost the election to Lloyd George in 1916 but remained leader of the

Churchill family graves at Bladon. (Newsquest Oxfordshire)

Liberal Party for a further ten years, after which he retired from politics to live at the Wharf, Sutton Courtenay.

The first of two famous men named William Morris (1834-1896) was born in Walthamstow in 1834, the third of nine children. While he was at Exeter College he started what was to become a life-time friendship with Edward Burne-Jones. Although he did not take a degree, Morris was offered the Professorship of Poetry; he refused but was made an honorary Fellow of Exeter College in 1883.

His time at Oxford increased Morris's interest in all things medieval and he came in to contact with like-minded people. Influenced by the works of Tennyson, Carlyle and Ruskin, Morris and his circle created their own version of the lost medieval world and filled it with art, furniture, furnishings, architecture and poetry according to the principles of their group, the Pre-Raphaelite Brotherhood.

The first William Morris. (Newsquest Oxfordshire)

George Orwell's grave at Sutton Courtenay. (Newsquest Oxfordshire)

Both Morris and Burne-Jones discarded their plans to be ordained in order to become artists, and Morris left Oxford in 1855. Two years later, together with a group which included Dante Gabriel Rossetti, the two friends painted the frescoes in the Old Library at the Oxford Union Society in St Michael Street, which were renovated in the late-twentieth century.

Morris's work was heavily influenced by that of Chaucer as well as the Icelandic sagas which he translated, and he also produced illuminated manuscripts similar to the medieval ones which he so admired.

Morris met the daughter of an ostler in Holywell, Jane Burden, who modelled for Rossetti and who appears in several Pre-Raphaelite paintings. He married Jane at St Michael at the North Gate Church in 1859, when she was only 20.

In the 1870s Morris and Rossetti took over the tenancy of Kelmscott Manor, a Tudor manor house by the Thames, where they lived from 1871 until Morris's death in 1896. Morris felt that it had 'grown out of the soil' with its 'quaint garrets amongst great timbers of the roof where of old times the tillers and herdsmen slept,' and this delighted him. Set into one of the walls at Kelmscott is a stone which shows tubby little Morris with his beard and mop of hair, sitting by his dovecote. Rossetti shared Jane as well as the Manor with William Morris.

The Morris family, William, Jane, who died in 1914, and their daughters Jane and May are buried in Kelmscott churchyard. Morris died in London in 1896 and was brought back to the village to be buried in a Viking-style tomb-house designed by Philip Webb. May Morris continued to live at the manor until 1938; the house was restored in 1963-6 and is open by appointment.

Oxfordshire's second William Morris, later Lord Nuffield, is buried in the churchyard of Holy Trinity Church, Nuffield, near Wallingford.

Another writer, Jerome Klapka Jerome (1859-1927), was born in Walsall, Staffordshire in 1859 but grew up in London's East End. During his working life he was a clerk, schoolmaster, reporter, actor and journalist before becoming joint editor of *The Idler* magazine in 1892, and starting his own weekly, *To-Day*. He is best remembered for *Three Men in a Boat* (1887), a book which follows the escapades of the author and his friends George, Harris and Montmorency the dog as they row their way up the Thames from Kingston upon Thames to Oxford, stopping off at a number of riverside towns and villages en route.

Jerome K. Jerome and his family lived at Gould's Grove (or Troy) an old farmhouse about 1.5 miles southeast of Ewelme. He is buried, together with his wife and daughter, under a stone which reads: 'For we are labourers together with God'.

The writer John Meade Falkner (1858-1932) was born in Manningford Bruce in Wiltshire, where his father was curate. In 1878 he went up to Hertford College to read Modern History, leaving with a Third Class degree. During his time at Oxford

Jerome K. Jerome's grave at Ewelme. (Newsquest Oxfordshire)

he learned several languages. He also explored Oxfordshire's towns and villages and grew to love Burford. After Falkner's death in 1932 his ashes were interred in the tomb of his brother, who had been buried in Burford churchyard in 1903. This bale tomb is the one to the furthest east of those in the churchyard.

Novelist and politician John Buchan, later 1st Baron Tweedsmuir, was born in 1875 and came up to Brasenose from Glasgow University and got a First in Classics in 1899. At the age of 52 he became Member of Parliament for the Scottish Universities and was created a baron in 1935, when he was appointed Governor General of Canada. Buchan lived at Elsfield Manor, just outside Oxford, and took his title from the village. After he died in 1940, he was cremated and his ashes brought back from Canada and buried under a circular stone in Elsfield churchyard.

Nancy Mitford was born in London in 1904, the eldest of seven children of Lord Redesdale, who owned houses at Astall and Swinbrook. Nancy's novels *The Pursuit of Love* (1945) and *Love in a Cold Climate* (1949), tell the family's life at Astall Manor and village and Swinbrook House. *Love in a Cold Climate* was made into a television film which was shot in the locality.

Nancy became the manager of a London bookshop during the Second World War, then moved to Paris in 1945. Her left-wing beliefs created a split among the upper-class Mitford family, some of whom disapproved of her mocking attitude towards the Establishment. The best-known of these is the idea of 'U' or 'non-U', that which is or is not socially acceptable. In addition to her novels and animated correspondence with her sisters and her close friend Evelyn Waugh, Nancy Mitford wrote historical biographies, notably of Madame de Pompadour (1954) and Frederick the Great (1970).

In 1967 Nancy moved to Versailles and at this period she began to suffer from an illness which proved to be Hodgkin's Disease. She never returned to England and died in France in June 1973. She was cremated at the Père Lachaise cemetery in Paris and her ashes were brought back to Swinbrook churchyard for burial near her sister, Unity. On Nancy's gravestone is a hedgehog as she did not like crosses. Unity Valkyrie Mitford, who died at Oban Cottage Hospital in 1948 at the age of 33, acquired a degree of notoriety for her friendship with Adolph Hitler.

The best-known works of George Orwell (1903-1950) include *Nineteen Eighty-Four* and *Animal Farm*. Orwell's real name was Eric Blair and he is buried at Sutton Courtenay. Blair specifically requested to be buried, according to rites of the Anglican Church, in an English country churchyard. David Astor, a long-standing friend of Orwell as well as his boss on the *Observer* newspaper, was able to arrange for Blair to be buried in a classic English country village as the Astor family owned the manor of Sutton Courtenay.

Born in Ulster in 1898, Clive Staples Lewis came up to University College in 1916. He got a First Class in Literae Humaniores in 1922 and in 1925 became a Fellow of Magdalen College. He shared a house called the Kilns, in Headington Quarry, with his brother, Warnie and the American writer Joy Gresham, whom he married in 1956. It was in the Kilns that he wrote some of his most famous works, including *The Lion, the Witch and the Wardrobe*. C.S. Lewis died on 22 November 1963 (the same day as Aldous Huxley), and is buried under a plain stone slab, decorated with only a cross, in the churchyard of Holy Trinity Church where he and Warnie had worshipped regularly.

Agatha Christie, the creator of fictional detectives Hercules Poirot and Miss Marple, was born in Torquay in Devon in 1890. Her second marriage in 1930 was to the archaeologist Sir Max Mallowan, whom she met on a dig in Iraq. Agatha Christie is reported to have remarked that this was the perfect profession for a husband because the older his wife became, the more interested he became in her! The Mallowans lived at Winterbrook House near Wallingford for many years and when she died in 1976 Agatha was buried in the churchyard at nearby Cholsey where she had worshipped for many years. Her grave is under a perimeter wall, a plot which she and Sir Max had chosen ten years before her death for their resting-place. The simple service included the hymns 'Holy, Holy, Holy,', 'The God of Love my Shepherd is', the 23rd Psalm and, at Dame Agatha's request, a reading from Edmund Spencer's *The Faerie Queen*. Along with the mourners were about twenty newspaper and television reporters, some having travelled from as far away as South America. The thirty wreaths included ones from the cast of her long-running play *The Mousetrap* and from the Savoy Theatre where another of her plays *Murder at the Vicarage* was playing. Flowers were sent by the Ulverscroft Large Print Book Publishers 'on behalf of the multitude of grateful readers'.

Agatha Christie's grave at Cholsey. (Newsquest Oxfordshire)

Another Oxonian who left an invaluable hoard of information about his life and times was Thomas Hearne (1678–1735) who came up to St Edmund Hall when he was seventeen and, like Anthony Wood, spent the remainder of his life in his college. Between 1705 and 1735 he filled 145 small notebooks with comments relevant to his position as scholar and librarian, much of the material concerning the history of the University. Following in Wood's footsteps he made himself unpopular with a number of prominent members of the university and had to live with the consequences. Lacking any sort of discretion in both his speech and his writings, he became known as an anti-Hanoverian troublemaker.

This did not prevent him from becoming Assistant Keeper of the Bodleian Library in 1701 and being promoted to Second Keeper in 1712 but in 1715, shortly after the accession of George I, he was 'debarr'd upon account of the oaths.' By refusing to take the obligatory oath of allegiance to the House of Hanover, he proved himself a Jacobite and as such, a security threat. When the Bodleian authorities changed the lock so that Hearne was not able to get into the library, he retired to his college where he prepared to publish the book on which he had been working for the last few years.

Hearne became Esquire Bedel in Law in January 1715 and he expected to be given the prestigious post of Printer to the University as his predecessors had been, but this was not to be. A nineteenth-century successor wrote that:

> Hearne did not long hold the [bedel's] staff, thus separated from the Press – he had made himself obnoxious by publishing Non-juror writings, and the Oaths of Allegiance, &c. stuck in his throat. He fell back upon the office of Under-Librarian at the Bodleian; but even there, his politics were turned against him. On being deprived of that post, he retired to a studious life in St Edmund Hall.

There, Hearne wrote many books on antiquities and in true Wood fashion toured round the country noting down everything that he saw.

Despite being criticized by Alexander Pope as 'Wormius, dry as dust,' it is the very remarks and prejudices that brought about his ruin that make Hearne such a useful and often humorous source for those researching everyday life in Georgian England. After he died on 20 June 1735 and was buried in the churchyard of St Peter in the East, more than £1,000 in cash was found in his room.

Early on the morning of 4 October 1784, James Sadler made aeronautical history by flying in a hot air balloon which he had made himself. This was unusual in itself but even more so considering that Sadler was a pastry cook and confectioner with a business in Oxford High Street. *Jackson's Oxford Journal* records how he set off in...

> ...his Fire Balloon, raised by means of rarefied air. The Process of filling the Globe began at three o'clock and about Half past Five as all was complete, and every Part of the Apparatus entirely adjusted, Mr Sadler, with Firmness and Intrepidity, ascended into the Atmosphere, and the Weather being calm and serene, he rose from the Earth in a vertical direction to a height of 3,600ft. In his elevated Situation he perceived no Inconvenience; and being disengaged from all terrestrial Things, he contemplated a most charming distant View. After floating for near Half an Hour, the machine descended, and at length came down upon a small Eminence betwixt Islip and Wood Eaton, about six Miles from this City.

On 12 November the same year, Sadler went up again, this time from the Botanic Garden and in a hydrogen balloon, watched by a very large crowd of spectators. He was quickly borne away across Otmoor and Thame. After seventeen minutes of flight, he made a very bumpy landing at Hartwell, just outside Aylesbury. The balloon blew into the branches of a tree and was ripped to pieces, but Sadler was uninjured.

The following year Sadler made four more ascents during which he was twice badly injured by being dragged along by the balloon. In October 1785, he was battered when he attempted to land at Lichfield and finally fell out when approaching the ground. The balloon itself promptly shot back heavenwards never to be seen again. This seems to have put him off ballooning temporarily, but in 1810 we find him, together with his son, Windham, rising from Merton Field in view of many members of the University. Trips from Birmingham to Boston and an ascent from Dublin followed.

James Sadler died a natural death in 1828 and was buried in the churchyard of St Peter in the East, where a plain gravestone has been erected to his memory by the Royal Aeronautical Society. Windham Sadler was less fortunate; when he was only 28, he collided with a chimney near Blackburn, the first death of an English aeronaut.

From the mid-sixteenth century onwards students reading medicine at Oxford were required to attend at least two human dissections before taking the degree of Bachelor of Medicine. Before they were allowed to practise, they were themselves obliged to perform a minimum of two dissections. This meant that for the first time medical men were obliged to both watch and perform dissections on human subjects.

The success of the teaching and study of human anatomy led to its own problems in obtaining sufficient material. After the Lent Assizes, the Reader was expected to get hold of, 'a Sounde body of one of the Executed persons,' if this were at all possible. This was not practicable during the summer months because of putrification and the required material was not forthcoming during Michaelmas Term, when there were no Assizes. Instead, the Reader gave lectures on the 'Sceleton or History of the bones with their Scituation Nature and Office'.

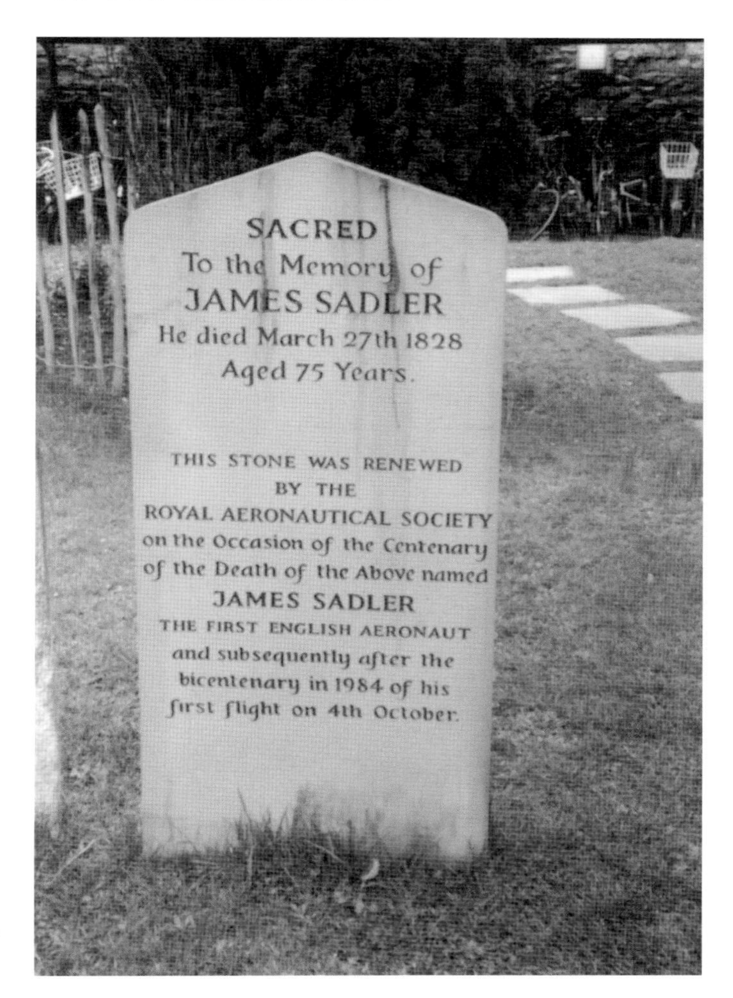

Aeronaut James Sadler's grave in the churchyard of St Peter in the East.

The source of corpses was increased by a charter of 1636 issued by Charles I that allowed the Reader to demand the body of any criminal executed within a 21-mile radius of the University.

To supplement the number of corpses legally available for dissection, body snatching took place throughout the country. Fresh corpses fetched a good price at anatomy schools despite the fact that anyone caught stealing a corpse might himself end up on the gallows. The theft of a corpse was not a crime, as it was not legally considered as property, although items such as shrouds were, and that is how many thieves were convicted. In addition, the public response to any interference with a dead body would have made a known perpetrator's life unbearable.

Oxfordshire's churchyards have several examples of the ways in which parishioners sought to protect their dead. One way was to build a watch house or

All Hallows' churchyard at Wallingford. (Newsquest Oxfordshire)

observation shed in which vigilantes could lie in wait after a burial until the corpse was too far decayed to be of any use. Other precautions were the use of a bottomless coffin-shaped box which was placed over the grave, construction of railings or an iron grille.

Jackson's Oxford Journal gives an account of a thwarted attempt at grave-robbing in March 1763:

> This week a set of Abandoned Miscreants were discovered in an attempt to rob a grave in Magdalen parish Churchyard in this City, in which the bodies of a woman and Infant had been interred two nights before. They were alarmed just as they were going to break the ground, upon which they took to their Heels and the bodies were next day taken up and re-interred in the Church to prevent any future attempt.

The passing of the Anatomy Act of 1832 was to make these precautions unnecessary.

St Mary Magdalen churchyard seems to have been something of a target for thieves, for in November 1772 a number of gravestones were stolen and presumably not recovered.

Any churchyard which has little connection with the living is always a potential headache for the local community unless it can be used for other purposes such as a relaxation area or as a wildlife haven. In 1976 a dispute arose over who was liable to pay for work done on the long-disused All Hallows' churchyard at Wallingford. When South Oxfordshire District Council took over the task of clearing the wilderness, workmen arrived with axes, saws and billhooks, but not long afterwards work came to a halt when the question of financing it was raised. The council believed that a precedent might be set and, to avoid becoming responsible for many other such overgrown churchyards under a section of the Local Government Act of 1972, invoked another section of the same Act to claim it as a 'special expense' payable by the town council. The town council asked South Oxfordshire to stop work, and so the churchyard remained overgrown.

Although it is neither an ancient parish churchyard nor one of the newer cemeteries, the plot where the ashes of a certain Mrs Carr are interred is one of the most prestigious in the country. Mrs Carr was college scout to J.R.R. Tolkien during his last years at Merton College and the site is under an ancient sycamore in the Fellows' garden, a favourite spot of the great man himself.

In the Newer Cemeteries

The situation regarding the opening of new cemeteries and the continuing use of older ones varied throughout the county and indeed still does. As regards the ancient parish churchyards, some remain open for burials, usually with at least one adjoining extension. Others are now closed but new ones have opened nearby, while yet others in Oxford and the larger towns have been long closed and new cemeteries opened at some distance from the centre of the community.

Chapels-of-ease, some of them centuries old, were opened in larger parishes to make it easier for worshippers to attend services without going miles to the parish church. These chapels had their own burial grounds but did not become parishes in their own right until the middle of the nineteenth century.

To cater for population expansion in Victorian times, new urban churches like St Paul's in Walton Street and St Barnabas in Canal Street, Oxford, were carved out of large old parishes, in this case St Thomas the Martyr. Initially St Paul's had no graveyard, which caused the churchwardens to write to the Trustees of the Radcliffe Infirmary on whose land St Paul's had been built. Their letter, dated 25 September 1838, survives in the National Health Service archives. The two churchwardens write requesting 'to be enabled to have the last solemn Christian service performed in the Church they frequented in life'; it is signed by the churchwardens and fifteen of the parishioners. They got their wish, but the burial ground has long been built over. Like St Paul's, other new town churches had short-lived graveyards, but others, like St Barnabas, never had one.

The history of burial grounds in Oxford, both parochial and municipal, is somewhat chequered. In the mid-nineteenth century, three new parish cemeteries were created: Osney at the end of Mill Street, off the Botley Road, Holywell off St Cross Road and St Sepulchre's in Walton Street. In addition, several small churches and chapels opened with their own burial plots.

Gothick canopies at Holywell.

The first of the three to open was Holywell, in 1847, and among those buried there are parishioners from the parishes of St Paul, St Mary Magdalen, St Giles, St Peter in the East, St Clement, St Mary the Virgin, St Aldate and Magdalen College, as well as numerous inmates of the Headington and Oxford workhouses.

The cemetery adjoins the old Holywell – or St Cross – churchyard, with which it should not be confused, and contains many interesting memorials, several to important members of the University. When it first opened concerns were expressed about the proximity of the water table to the surface and horror stories abounded regarding water-filled graves, floating coffins which refused to be submerged and waterlogged corpses. Whether this was a case of overactive imaginations running wild or one exception being made the rule, it is certain that the grieving families of professors and heads of colleges would not have considered burial at Holywell cemetery for an instant if there had been even the remotest possibility of this happening to their dearly departed.

Along the boundary wall are Gothick canopies and angels, copied from some in the Church of St Mary the Virgin. The wall tablet's inscription JWB stands for Dr John William Burgon, who is buried there with other members of the Burgon family. On the north-facing wall, between the garden of Holywell Manor and

This memorial to the Poulton Palmer family incorporates a restored wooden cross which was brought from the grave of Ronald William Poulton Palmer, a Lieutenant in the Royal Berkshire Regiment, who is buried at Ploegsteert, where he was killed in 1915. A Balliol man, he was captain of the England Rugby XV in 1914. Other Poultons in Holywell are Sir Edward Bagnall Poulton (1856-1943), Hope Professor of Zoology; Emily Palmer Poulton, who was the daughter of George Palmer who founded Huntley & Palmer's biscuit-manufacturing business and Edward Palmer Poulton, who held the position of Senior Physician at Guy's Hospital. The ill-fated Ronald William had been adopted by George Palmer and was expected to take over the business.

This very unusual terracotta memorial is that of Sir John Rhŷs, an outstanding Celtic scholar and champion of Welsh and Irish culture, who was born John Rees in Cardiganshire in 1840. He came up to Jesus College in 1865, took a First in Classics in 1869 and became a Fellow of Merton College the same year. When the Jesus Chair of Celtic was founded at Oxford in 1877 he was elected its first professor and honorary fellow of Jesus College. After serving as Bursar, he was elected Principal of Jesus in 1895; he was knighted in 1907. He died at the Principal's Lodgings on 17 December 1915, and was buried on 23 December.

Holywell cemetery, stone tablets record Burgon burials in vaults in the cemetery itself. John Burgon was born in Smyrna, where his father was a merchant and a member of the Levant Company, in 1813. The family moved back to England and John matriculated as a member of Worcester College in 1841, took his BA in 1845 and won the Newdigate Prize for English verse with the poem 'Petra' that summer. It includes the couplet:

> Match me such marvel, save in eastern clime,
> A rose-red city half as old as time.

which drew down on Burgon's head accusations of plagiarism from its similarity to Samuel Rogers' use of the line 'By many a temple half as old as time', in the poem *Italy*.

He became the incumbent of the University church, where he stayed for twelve years, opposing all sorts of people and attacking popular causes and beliefs. One of his fixations was about the place of women in the University, a concept which he attacked both from the pulpit and in print, making himself a figure of ridicule in the process. In 1875 he was given the position of Dean of Chichester, where he soon made himself unpopular by his sharp and inflexible attitude to his colleagues. Despite living in Sussex, Burgon continued to meddle in the affairs of Oxford University and once more made himself a laughing-stock by his criticism of the lodging-house system, which he saw as being potentially dangerous to the morals of the young. An invitation to Burgon to sit on a parliamentary commission for university reform met with such violent protest that he was obliged to withdraw. Notwithstanding his arrogant behaviour, those who knew Burgon in his private life found him a warm and loyal friend and, although fond of children and women provided they remained in their 'right place', he never married. He died in the Deanery at Chichester in 1888 and his body was brought to Oxford for burial in the family grave a week later.

An Oxford tradesman with a rather strange claim to fame is Theophilus Carter who had a hat-making business on the north side of the High Street, between Queen's Lane and Longwall Street. Lewis Carroll is thought to have portrayed him as the Mad Hatter who presides over Alice's tea-party. Hatters used mercury in their work and this is said to have affected their brains. Mad or sane, Carter died in 1904 and lies in Holywell cemetery with his 1-year-old granddaughter.

Kenneth Grahame was born in Edinburgh in 1859, but was brought up by relatives after his mother died in 1864, and went to St Edward's School in North Oxford. Ratty, Badger, Mole and Toad originated in a series of bedtime stories and letters written for Grahame's son, Alistair. Although they were not intended for publication, they appeared as a complete story, *The Wind in the Willows*, in 1908. The book is set around the River Thames; Mapledurham House is said to feature as Toad Hall and the original illustrations by E.H. Shepard suggest that this might indeed be the case.

The Wind in the Willows was dramatised by A.A. Milne in 1930 as *Toad of Toad Hall.* In the play Toad sings immodestly:

> The clever men at Oxford,
> Know all there is to be knowed,
> But none of them knows one half as much,
> As intelligent Mr Toad.

Between 1910 and 1924, Kenneth Grahame lived in a Tudor farmhouse called Bohan's in the village of Blewbury, in the Vale of White Horse. Kenneth and Alistair

Grahame are buried in one grave, to the right of the pathway on entering Holywell cemetery; Kenneth's epitaph, written by Anthony Hope Hawkins, which is on the nearside of the gravestone, speaks of 'the beautiful memory' of Grahame.

Kenneth Tynan was born in Birmingham in 1927. He came up to Magdalen College where, as his entry in the *Dictionary of National Biography* puts it, 'he embarked upon a systematic campaign to outshine or outrage all contemporaries as undergraduate journalist, actor, impresario, party-giver, and [despite a stammer] debater.'

After working for a short time as a director in repertory theatre, Tynan became a professional theatre critic. One of his claims to fame is that in 1965 he has gone on record as the first Briton to use the 'F word' on television. He was diagnosed with emphysema the same year. Besides being a critic, he wrote for the theatre and is probably best known for the nude scenes in the revue *Oh! Calcutta!*, which appeared first in New York in 1969, and then in London; it became a success wherever it was shown. Tynan's entry in *Who's Who* lists his interests as sex and eating.

His illness caused him to move to California and he died in Los Angles on 26 July 1980. He was cremated and his ashes were brought back to Britain to be interred in Holywell cemetery that September.

Osney cemetery was opened in 1848 on a brown-field site which had once formed part of the extensive Osney Abbey. It was used by the poorer parishes to the west and south-west of the city and never attained the status of either Holywell or St Sepulchre.

St Sepulchre's cemetery opened in 1850 on a site adjacent to Lucy's iron foundry in Walton Well Road and there was a saying among those living nearby that they would prefer not to be buried at St Sepulchre's for fear of their 'skellingtons' being 'all joggled about' by the reverberations from the works. Of those who are interred here, the best known is Benjamin Jowett, although many of the others were minor celebrities in their day. St Sepulchre's is a typical example of a mid-Victorian cemetery for it has no cult burials to which visitors make a pilgrimage as at Holywell, Wolvercote and Holy Trinity Headington Quarry. It is not a showplace but neither has it been left to decay.

Benjamin Jowett came up to Balliol on a scholarship in 1836 from St Paul's School and stayed there for the rest of his life. He was a classical scholar and worked on the New Testament, attracting strong criticism from some quarters for his remark that the New Testament should be studied 'like any other book'. He was also very much involved in university reform, and taking full advantage of the resulting improvement in the standard of scholarship, Jowett succeeded in making Balliol the centre of academic excellence, which it is to this day. Religious and academic considerations aside, it is Jowett's friendship with Florence Nightingale and their extensive correspondence which is of interest to the layman. She turned down his

Kenneth Grahame's grave in Oxford's Holywell cemetery.

Kenneth Tynan's grave in Oxford's Holywell cemetery.

The grave of Benjamin Jowett, Master of Balliol from 1870 to 1893. (Newsquest Oxfordshire)

Opposite from top:
Encouraged by the Revd A. Mallinson, vicar of St Frideswide's Church in Botley Road, these theology students from St Stephen's House are shown clearing Osney cemetery of grass and weeds in 1955. (Newsquest Oxfordshire)

Five years later the situation at Osney had not improved much. A press photographer was sent there in August 1960 and the resulting picture used for a report which stated, misleadingly, that the cemetery was due to be closed. It had in fact been closed for burials since 1946. The article also claimed that, 'Bishops, a Count of the Holy Roman Empire, a Knight of the Order of the Redeemer of Greece, former City Fathers, tradesmen and tramps are among those whose graves are in Osney Cemetery,' the last three categories of resident are correct but the first three refer to burials in Osney Abbey, not in the Victorian cemetery. The caretaker's cottage had been condemned as uninhabitable by the time this photograph was taken. (Newsquest Oxfordshire)

proposal of marriage and he remained unwed. He suffered from a succession of serious illnesses from 1887 onwards and died on 1 October 1893. A funeral service was held in the college chapel and crowds turned out for the occasion. Seven Balliol graduates who went on to become heads of other colleges carried his coffin to the grave.

In November 1984 the *Oxford Times* carried an article about a so-called 'dead-letter' box in St Sepulchre's. One of the graves there features in Chapman Pincher's spy novel, *Too Secret Too Long* (1984). The book's setting is Oxfordshire, and in it Pincher claims that this grave was used for depositing espionage documents for exchange during the Cold War.

St Sepulchre's has numerous other examples of full-size and miniature headstones marking the same grave. At first glance the smaller ones appear to be foot-stones which have been moved, but there are too many for this to be the case and it will be seen that they commemorate children.

In 1878 the churchyard of the new church of SS Mary and John in Oxford's Cowley Road was opened to cater for the expanding population of East Oxford. By 1947 there was no more room for any further burials, except for those of

This photograph of the interior of the closed chapel at St Sepulchre's, taken in June 1971, is very evocative of desolation and decay. With the sunlight pouring through the holes in the roof, the chapel looks like a medieval ruin although the glass is still intact, the bier is in place and the Bible has been left open after the last service to take place there. (Newsquest Oxfordshire)

'Dead-letter' box in St Sepulchre's cemetery. (Newsquest Oxfordshire)

people who had booked their grave, or who were going to be interred with family members. The churchyard of SS Mary and John was formally closed for burials in 2000, although cremated ashes may still be buried there. It is estimated that between 1879 and 2000, more than 2,000 burials took place there, including those of infants, patients from the asylum at Littlemore and from the workhouse, whose graves are unmarked.

Before the County Pauper Lunatic Asylum at Littlemore was provided with its own burial ground, 'patients whose families did not provide for burial' had been interred in the parish churchyard at Littlemore, which placed a serious burden on its resources. The asylum ground was extended in 1900, the last burial there took place in 1954 and the hospital itself closed in 1996. A strange series of events concerning burial markers took place at Littlemore. The archives of Oxfordshire Mental Healthcare NHS Trust contain a number of envelopes marked with 'Return to Sender' or other similar comments and were duly returned unopened. They had been sent to the families of patients who died in the asylum and, because they are black-edged, it was obvious what news they contained. When patients had no friends or family who would bear the cost of the funeral they were buried in a paupers' graves. An influential and well-meaning visitor complained that there were no memorial stones in the graveyard, the reason being that these were very expensive and beyond the means of many working people, let alone paupers. As a compromise, metal crosses were erected and these remained in place until an enterprising gardener removed them, his reason being, no doubt, that they were more suitable for a scrapyard than a graveyard.

In 1889, because of pressure on the existing ones, the newly-formed Oxford Corporation bought land for municipal cemeteries outside the city boundaries at Wolvercote and Rose Hill. Rose Hill cemetery (11 acres), which was dedicated in 1892, remains open for burials and is a typical, modern suburban cemetery, pleasant in itself but not noteworthy. Wolvercote cemetery, a 13-acre site lying to the west of the main road at Cutteslowe, was also dedicated in 1892. It is undoubtedly the most interesting of the Oxford cemeteries which are still open for burials. Although a single unit, it is divided into areas where graves of Oxford's various religious and ethnic communities can be located, notably Jewish, Muslim, Baha'i Faith, Roman Catholic, Greek and Russian Orthodox, as well as those of no religious affiliation.

The novelist Dorothy L. Sayers is also buried at Wolvercote. A plaque on No. 1 Brewer Street, St Aldates, marks her birthplace in 1893. After taking a First in French from Somerville in 1915 her first job in publishing was at Blackwell's, where she was eventually sacked by Sir Basil Blackwell himself.

Sayers' best-loved work is the detective series featuring Lord Peter Wimsey, the first of which was *Whose Body?* published in 1923. Another of her novels, *Busman's Honeymoon*, mentions St Cross Church in Holywell, and the popular

Gaudy Night (1935) was made into a film. In addition to detective fiction, Sayers produced translations of Dante's *Inferno* and *Purgatorio*, which were published in 1949 and 1955.

The writer's significant comment on twentieth-century literature, which appeared in *That's Why I Never Read Modern Novels*, is:

> As I grow older and older,
> And totter towards the tomb,
> I find that I care less and less
> Who goes to bed with whom.

Dorothy L. Sayers died in 1957.

Another Oxford literary giant whose grave is in Wolvercote cemetery is John Ronald Reuel Tolkien, who was born in South Africa in 1892 but came to England when he was 7.

He came up to Exeter College in 1908, was awarded the College's open Classical Exhibition in 1910, took a Second in Classics Moderations in 1913 and a First in English Language and Literature two years later.

Tolkien was sent to France in 1916, shortly after his marriage to Edith Bratt, and their son John was born in 1917. At the end of the war the Tolkiens returned to Oxford where they lived at 50 St John Street before moving to 1 Alfred Street.

In 1920, he left Oxford to take up a post at the University of Leeds, where he became Professor of English Language in 1924, but returned to Oxford the following year when he was appointed to the Rawlinson and Bosworth Professorship of Anglo-Saxon at Pembroke College.

The Tolkiens lived at several addresses in Oxford before settling in 20 Northmoor Road, where they stayed for seventeen years. This house has one of the few blue plaques in Oxford.

The Hobbit, the companion and forerunner of *The Lord of the Rings* trilogy, was published in 1937, followed by *The Fellowship of the Ring* in 1954, *The Two Towers* in 1955 and *The Return of the King* the following year.

In 1945 Tolkien was elected Merton Professor of English Language and Literature and moved college from Pembroke to Merton. The family moved to a Merton property, 3 Manor Road, where they lived for three years until they moved to 99 Holywell Street, another Merton property.

From 1953 until 1968, the Tolkiens lived at 76 Sandfield Road, Headington, as a plaque above the garage states. Tolkien retired in 1959 and in 1968 they moved to Bournemouth. When Edith died there in 1971, Tolkien returned to Oxford and lived at 21 Merton Street until his death in 1973 while in Bournemouth on holiday. He was buried with Edith, and on the gravestone is the inscription:

The grave of John Ronald Reuel Tolkien and his wife Edith.

EDITH MARY TOLKIEN
LUTHIEN
1889–1971
JOHN RONALD REUEL TOLKIEN
BEREN
1892–1973

Other notable burials at Wolvercote cemetery include philosopher Sir Isaiah Berlin; historian Peter Laslett; historian Geoffrey Lewis, an authority on Turkish studies; and the poet Elizabeth Jennings.

The grave of Sir Isaiah Berlin, philosopher and first Warden of Wolfson College, who died in 1997 and is buried in the Jewish section of the cemetery.

In 1890 the Oxford Corporation bought land for a third municipal cemetery, which was dedicated in the same year: this was an 8-acre site at Botley. In addition to the graves of Oxford citizens, the cemetery at Botley now contains 156 burials of casualties of the First World War, all of which are in the war graves plot in section I/1. Virtually all of the 516 Second World War burials, including one of an unidentified person, are in the extended war graves plot. As well as the war graves of personnel from the Commonwealth, the cemetery contains almost seventy war graves of other nationalities. These are not confined to members of the Allied Forces such as French or Poles, but also Germans and Italians. The cemetery is the venue for a moving Service of Remembrance in November each year.

Headington did not become part of the city of Oxford until 1928 and that same year its parish council cemetery became a public burial ground for the whole city. Like Wolvercote, Headington remains open for burials and contains some interesting graves, although few of national importance.

An example of a provincial Victorian town cemetery is given in this description of Abingdon cemetery from Kelly's directory of 1902:

> The cemetery is in the Spring Road, west of the town, and consists of about six acres, prettily laid out and planted; there are two mortuary chapels of stone, in the decorated style, and a curator's residence. The Cemetery is under the control of a joint committee of 10 members, appointed by the Urban District Council of Abingdon and the Parish meeting [vestry board] for St Helen's Without.

Opposite from top:
This photograph, taken in 1956, shows Air Marshall Sir Charles Guest, a member of the Imperial War Graves Commission, visiting Botley cemetery to inspect the graves of servicemen and women, which Oxford City Council maintains on behalf of the Commission. (Newsquest Oxfordshire)

The first burial in this small private cemetery in Bicester took place in 1897. The name of the deceased was Watchman and on his gravestone is a quotation from Addison. In all, there were twenty-two burials, the last being that of King David in 1948. Other graves are those of King John, Princess Mary, Queen Elizabeth, King William and even Don Quixote, with epitaphs from the Iliad, Byron, Shakespeare and the Bible. These are the graves of dogs (and at least one cat) belonging to a Mrs Keith-Falconer, who was very fond of foxhounds. (Newsquest Oxfordshire)

Into an Early Grave

The life-span of earlier generations was usually much shorter than it is nowadays. Apart from general causes such as war, accidents, disease, poor nutrition and occasionally actual starvation, there are other reasons for people going to their graves earlier than might be expected. Among these were childbirth, suicide, murder and execution, loose living, harsh weather conditions and unexplained factors which were simply noted as being an 'Act of God'. Injuries and accidents were of course very common and many deaths could have been avoided if efficient health and safety procedures had been followed. Similarly, diseases which seem relatively minor to us proved fatal to our ancestors.

High infant mortality was common until well into the twentieth century, even among the middle and upper classes – as shown by the entries in the county's parish burial registers. The Ewelme burial register records the demise of 'John Howard of Charlton, son of Charles, Lord Viscount Adiwer' (Andover), in 1663. He has an epitaph by Edmund Waller which runs:

Tis no wonder Death our hopes beguiled.
He's seldom old that will not be a child.

In the churchyard at Stanford-in-the-Vale, Henry and Mary Willis erected a stone to their son William, who died in 1827 aged 12. It reads:

Our life hangs by a single thread
Which soon is cut and we are dead
Then boast not reader of thy might
Alive at noon and dead at night.

Two Thame parents were mourning 2-year-old Robert and two-day-old Mary, their 'children deare'. (Newsquest Oxfordshire)

In the same churchyard the oldest legible stone, which dates from 1680, reads:

> Here Lyeth
> Ann White Dafter
> of Richard White
> Who deceased the
> 7 Day of November
> A Maiden Faire A Jew-
> ell Rare a Virgin Pure
> Her Fathers Staff
> Her Mothers Stay.

Closely associated with infant mortality, whether cause or effect, was death in childbirth. An unusual brass on the wall of St Cross Church shows Mrs Elizabeth Franklin, aged 35, sitting up in bed in her home, which was the King's Arms on the corner of Holywell Street and Parks Road, where her husband, Thomas, was landlord. On the bed coverlet are four dead babies, three bundled in shrouds and one wrapped in swaddling clothes, with the words 'of such / are the / kingdome / of heaven' written alongside them. Elizabeth has her hands together in prayer, and the words, 'Thy will be done' are coming from her mouth and rising up to heaven. From three winged figures in heaven float back the reassuring words: 'Thy prayere is heard'; 'Receave thy crowne'; and 'Thy patience is tri'd'.

Elizabeth joined her four dead children in heaven on 31 July 1622. The inscription accompanying the brass reads:

> Here lyeth Eliza: Franklin third wife of Mr Tho: Franklin who dangerously escaping death at 3 severall travells in childe-bed, died together wth the fourth July 31: Aetat: 35: 1622
> If heavens inheritors on earth be tride,
> that thou art one of them, thou need'st not feare
> What thou indur'dst these dead have testify'd
> and thus being try'de a crowne deserv'st to weare
> Lett then thy husbands children cease their woe
> thou left's them only to thine owne to goe.

As a county, Oxfordshire has been lucky in that it has been relatively unaffected by war, having seen no major battles and suffered no invasions or air raids. Apart from the ones at Botley, burial records of soldiers are few and date mainly from the Civil Wars of the 1640s.

One of the most impressive funerals must have been that of Lord Aubigny, a casualty of the Battle of Edgehill in October 1642 and who was buried in the cathedral in January 1643. Anthony Wood notes in his diary:

> Friday 13 Jan., a great solemne funeral in Oxon of Lord Aubigny (brother to the duke of Lennox) who was slaine at kaynton field or at the battell of Edgehill. The body was brought up from MagdalenCollege and so brought and attended all the way through the street to Christchurch the Cathedrall, and there entered. The footmen soldiers came first with their muskets under their armes, the noses of the muskets being behind them; the pike men drayled their pikes on the ground: the horsemen followed with their pistols in their hands, the handles being upwarde; the tops of the auntients also was borne behind. A chariot covered with black velevett, where the body was drawen by 6 horses, &c. The man that drove the chariot strowed money about the streets as he passed Three great volleys of shot at the enterring of the body; and lastly, an herald of armes proclaimed his titles.

A questionable death was that of Lucius Cary, Lord Falkland, whose effigy can be seen in miniature on his grandparents' tomb in Burford church, although he is not

The Coates family of Thame were especially unlucky when they lost Merriel and Simon within weeks of each other, as these plaques on the wall of the choir show.

buried there with them. Falkland was killed at Newbury in September 1643 when he galloped ahead of his troops, straight towards enemy musketeers, and received a fatal shot in the abdomen. Witnesses called his behaviour 'scarcely distinguishable from suicide', caused, it was said, by his horror of the conflict which was tearing the country apart. His corpse, found the following day 'stript, trod upon and mangled' and identified only by a mole on the neck, was taken into the town, then on to Oxford and finally back to his home at Great Tew. Falkland was buried in the chancel of St Michael's Church in an unmarked grave for fear of later desecration. His wife and three sons were subsequently buried there with him but it was not until the end of the nineteenth century that the squire put up a monument to him.

Troops fighting on either side of the conflict are occasionally mentioned singly or in very small numbers in burial registers throughout the county, like the Royalist troopers buried in the churchyard at Stanford in the Vale. In the majority of cases these soldiers were unknown to the parishioners and probably died in skirmishes or from wounds or disease.

Charles I was beheaded in January 1649 and in the May of that year a mutiny arose in the ranks of the Parliamentarian army. Some of the rebels, who came to be known as 'Levellers' because they sought more social equality, reached Burford on the evening of 13 May, hotly pursued by Fairfax and Cromwell. The soldiery bedded down in billets around the town and posted few sentries.

During the night they were caught up in a two-pronged attack from Fairfax on one side and Cromwell on the other. Two men were killed and about 340 of the rebels taken prisoner. These were herded into the parish church, where they spent three nights until it was decided what should happen to them. A souvenir of their stay is the inscription 'Anthony Sedley 1649 Prisner', which can still be seen carved into the lead rim of the font.

A swift court-martial was arranged, the outcome of which was that three so-called ringleaders should be taken outside, put against the church wall and shot. This happened in view of the remainder of the prisoners, who were marched up to the roof to watch. In the Burford parish registers is an entry to the effect that three soldiers had been 'shot to death'. Bullet marks can still be seen, and a plaque set into the south wall reads: 'To the Memory of Three Levellers Cornet Thompson, Corporal Perkins and Private Church. Executed and buried in this Churchyard 17th May 1649'.

A similar plaque on a wall in Oxford's Gloucester Green reads:

TO THE MEMORY OF Private BIGGS and Private PIGGEN EXECUTED LIKE THEIR LEVELLER COLLEAGUES AT BURFORD BY FORCED LOYAL TO CROMWELL. THEY WERE SHOT NEAR THIS PLACE FOR THEIR PART IN THE SECOND MUTINY OF THE OXFORD GARRISON ON 18TH SEPTEMBER 1649.

Murder, either by violence or by more subtle methods, was by no means uncommon. A slab set into the sanctuary steps of the University Church of St Mary the Virgin, High Street, Oxford, relates that, 'in a vault of brick, at the upper end of the quire of this church, lie the mortal remains of Amy Robsart'. Amy was the wife of Lord Robert Dudley, afterwards Earl of Leicester, Chancellor of the University, and a favourite of Queen Elizabeth. In 1560, Amy was found lying at the foot of the stairs at her home, Cumnor Hall, with a broken neck. Foul play was suspected but never proved as Amy was buried too hurriedly for the coroner to give a verdict. She was exhumed on her lord's instructions with a great show of grief. Before being reburied in St Mary's on 22 September, Amy lay in state in Gloucester Hall, in what is now part of Worcester College, and is reputed to haunt the Junior Common Room there.

Under a black marble slab in Burford church lie the remains of John Pryor, whose inscription reads:

> Here Lyeth the body of
> JOHN PRYOR GENT who was
> murdered and found hidden in the priory Garden in this
> parish the 3 day of April
> Anno Domini 1697 and was
> Buried the 6th day of the same
> month in the 67 yeare
> of his age.

In eighteenth-century Henley-on-Thames, Mary Blandy, the lady at the centre of a murder trial, was not the victim but the murderer. She was found guilty of administering poison to her father. The following account comes from the *The Complete Newgate Calendar*:

> At the ensuing assizes at Oxford Miss Blandy was indicted for the wilful murder of her father, and was immediately found guilty upon the confession which she had made. She addressed the jury at great length, repeating the story which she had before related; but all was of no avail, and sentence of death was passed. At nine in the morning of the 6th of April, 1752, she left her apartment to be conducted to the scaffold, habited in a black bombasine dress, her arms being bound with black ribands.
>
> On her ascending the gallows she begged that she might not be hanged high, 'for the sake of decency'; and on her being desired to go a little higher, expressed her fear that she should fall. The rope having been put round her neck, she pulled her handkerchief over her face, and was turned off on holding out a book of devotions which she had been reading.

Leveller plaque at Burford.

A feature of this execution was that the gallows were not of the type usually portrayed in pictures of executions, but were constructed by two young trees being bent over and lashed together.

When Mary's body was cut down, there was nothing ready to put it in and it was carried through the crowd on the shoulders of one of the Sheriff's men as if it were a carcase of meat, as an eyewitness put it. It was kept for some hours at this man's house.

Arrangements were then made for her to be brought back home to Henley. At one o'clock on the morning of Tuesday 7 April she was buried, as she had asked, in the parish church there, between her father and mother.

In spite of the ceremony taking place at night, 'there was assembled the greatest concourse of people ever known upon such an occasion.' Henley parish church has been altered since then, and Mary Blandy's grave is now unmarked, although it is thought to be beneath the organ in the north choir aisle.

If she had been executed a matter of weeks afterwards, Mary Blandy's end might have been even less dignified. Due to a disturbing increase in the number of murders, an Act was passed 'for better preventing the Horrid Crime of Murder'. Accordingly, condemned persons should be executed the next day but one after sentence, and their bodies be given to the Surgeons' Company for dissection; at the discretion of the judge, they might be hanged in chains. The first person to whom this applied died on 1 July 1752.

Just outside the west door of St Mary's parish church in Thame is the Edden family grave. It is another memorial which records a murder. On the night of 25 October 1828, as William Noble Edden, a 65-year-old market gardener, was walking to his home in Thame through the village of Haddenham, he was killed. Although his body was not found until the following morning his wife had a vision in which his apparition informed her that he had been attacked and left in a ditch. She told her astounded neighbours that she had even seen the murderer, a man called Benjamin Tyler.

When apprehended, Tyler vehemently denied the accusations and no further action could be taken due to lack of more substantial evidence. Several months later, though, a labourer named Solomon Sewell told magistrates that he had seen Tyler hit Edden with a hammer, but because Sewell was mentally retarded, his account was dismissed. In 1830 however, Tyler was re-arrested and sent for trial along with Sewell. This time they were both found guilty and executed at Aylesbury in front of an estimated crowd of 5,000 people who had turned up in front of the prison to watch. Sewell's corpse was taken away to be dissected at St Bartholomew's Hospital in London. Afterwards, the surgeons stated that his brain showed signs of disease and indicated that he might well have been insane, probably from birth.

William Edden's ghost is said to haunt the place on the road from Aylesbury to Thame where the murder took place. His grave is also said to be haunted, not by Edden himself but by a ram-like animal, which trots along behind passers-by.

On Friday 24 May 2002, the Bishop of Oxford, the Right Reverend Richard Harries, took a service in Oxford Gaol's cemetery. The *Oxford Mail* quotes Claire Sandford, the instigator of the idea, as saying, 'When I was taken on a tour of the prison site I was struck by the distressed feeling of the place. We all talk about these issues, but this made it seem so very real.' Some thirty criminals executed at the prison lie there in unmarked graves.

The Bishop's blessing took place almost half a century after the death of the last man to be hanged at Oxford Castle.

One of the reasons that certain members of Oxfordshire society went early to their graves was suicide, which remained illegal until 1961. Anthony Wood records a good number of seventeenth-century examples, the two principal causes being unrequited love and unwanted pregnancy. Hanging and drowning were the usual methods. On 23 October 1681, for example, William Cardinall, a Fellow of Merton College, hanged himself on his bedroom door, wearing only his shirt and night-cap. About 11 o'clock that same night he was buried stark naked in the vestry yard on the south side of the chancel of the college chapel.

The Edden family grave at St Mary's parish church in Thame.

On one of the pillars in the cathedral is the coloured bust of Robert Burton (1577–1640), who was born in Leicestershire and in 1593 came up to Brasenose, where his elder brother was already a student. He migrated to Christ Church, where he was elected a Student (a Fellow) of that college in 1599, although he did not receive his BA until 1602. He took charge of the college library and spent the remainder of his life at Christ Church, although he was also vicar of the West Oxford church of St Thomas the Martyr from 1616 until his death.

Burton is remembered for his work *The Anatomy of Melancholy* (subtitled 'What it is, With all the kinds, causes, symptomes, prognostickes, and severall cures of it'), which was published in 1621 under the *nom de plume* of Democritus Junior, and was extended and amended several times in Burton's lifetime. Its purpose was to distract Burton from his own melancholy, but in this it failed dismally. Later writers, including Sterne, Lamb, Coleridge and Milton, used the book and Samuel Johnson said that *Anatomy* was the only one which could get him out of bed two hours before he wanted to.

Burton never married and Anthony Wood, who knew him well, writes that he used astrological calculations to predict the time of his own death. When the hour came on 25 January 1640, says Wood, Burton hanged himself and so made his prediction come true.

Reports in *Jackson's Oxford Journal* suggest that in the second half of the eighteenth century suicides were not uncommon; there were three in 1786 and again in 1787, and four the following year.

Oxford Gaol cemetery.

When these deaths are checked with entries in the parish burial registers it is apparent that the way in which this problem was dealt with differs considerably from case to case. Not only was suicide a crime, it was thought at one time to damn the offender's immortal soul. If the family was a respected one, the local community frequently conspired to spare them the stigma of having one of its members being buried in unconsecrated ground.

A sympathetic coroner and jury would return a verdict of 'Insane', or more frequently 'Lunacy'. This would permit burial in the churchyard as, being of unsound mind, the deceased had not been not responsible for his or her own actions. Sometimes the individual is not mentioned in the register at all, but more frequently the burial is recorded with no comment to indicate the cause of death. One such was Elizabeth Jarvis of Garsington, who managed to drown herself at the second attempt in 1781 but was nevertheless buried in her parish churchyard.

An unusual and less obvious kind of self-destruction was recorded in 1755, when an inquest was taken at Thame on the body of Richard Godding, an 80-year-old labourer from Great Haseley who died after eating an exceptionally large meal. No will was found, and no relative known, so he was buried by the parish.

More dramatic suicides and their consequences were covered by *Jackson's Oxford Journal*. In July 1782 it reported a criminal named Haddon who had been condemned to death for robbing the mail, was found dead in the condemned cell in Oxford castle. He had used the traditional method of tying his bed sheets to the bars at the window in order to escape, but did this by hanging himself. An inquest was held and the verdict *felo de se* was returned. Haddon was buried the next day in the Botley turnpike road, apparently a favourite spot for disposing of suicides. However, there was an additional twist to this tale for his friends came along later, opened the grave and filled it up with lime in order to prevent the corpse being taking off for dissection.

In 1787 another inquest was held at Thame, this time on the body of William Burnard. The deceased was discovered hanging in a hayloft. The verdict was 'wilful murder on himself' and the body ordered to be buried in the public highway.

At Assendon Cross near Henley-on-Thames, an inquest was held the following year on the body of an unnamed man aged about 22. He had gone to work in the woods as usual on a Friday morning, a week before Christmas. His father found him the next day 'suspended by his garter on a bough of a tree, dead.' The jury's verdict was 'Self Murder' and this young man was also buried in the public highway. In 1823 an Act was passed forbidding this practise and directing that suicides be buried in a churchyard; the only reservations were that this was to take place without rites and only between the hours of 9 p.m. and midnight.

In Dorchester Abbey, near the font, is a slab commemorating Sarah Fletcher, who died 'of excessive Sensibility' in 1799. Sarah's story is much more interesting than this indicates. She was a sea captain's wife who lived nearby at Clifton Hampden, and on learning that her husband had attempted to marry an heiress she hanged herself from her bed rail with a handkerchief attached to a piece of cord. In order that she might be given a Christian burial, the coroner returned the charitable verdict of lunacy. Her burial entry for 10 May in the Clifton Hampden register makes no mention of suicide.

Nevertheless, there are many well-authenticated stories about the appearance of Sarah's ghost; she has long red hair and wears a swirling black velvet cloak. A nineteenth-century resident at her former home found Sarah so attractive that he fell in love with her, and looked forward eagerly to her visits. Late-twentieth-century accounts in the local press tell of Sarah peering through the windows of vehicles left in the car park of the Barley Mow at Clifton Hampden.

The slab in Dorchester Abbey commemorating Sarah Fletcher. (Newsquest Oxfordshire)

Although the most sensational of the inquests that coroners were required to conduct concerned suicides or suspicious deaths, the vast majority of cases were the victims of misfortune and the verdict returned was Accidental Death or, less frequently, Act of God. A return for 1837 gives the corner's expenses at that time to be a pound for each inquest conducted plus travelling expenses at 9*d* a mile to be paid out of the County rate. Jurymen 'generally' received 8*d* each and the Constable was paid 'according to the distance in going after the Witnesses.'

A very ordinary headstone in Stoke Lyne churchyard marks the burial place of Emily Ermyntrude Bryant. At the base of the cross is an inscription in lead lettering which reads,

> In loving memory of Emily Ermyntrude, the beloved daughter of the Rev. William Bryant, MA, Vicar of this parish, who died February 5, 1906, aged 14 years.
> The damsel is not dead but sleepeth.

However, the middle section of the inscription has been removed. This used to read:

> her premature death was partly caused by a bitter boycott and persecution organised by persons of position and influence in this parish.

In the early years of the twentieth century a double tragedy shook this little village in the north of Oxfordshire.

Emily's father, the Revd Bryant, became vicar in 1892 having the reputation of being an outstanding scientist. He treated his wife so badly that, ten years later, she left him to bring up Emily, their only child. Leading parishioners sided with Mrs Bryant, and this created a very unpleasant atmosphere, and culminated in a boycott of church services headed by the squire, Sir Algernon Peyton.

Emily was the innocent victim of this feud; she had remained on very affectionate terms with her father despite all that had happened within the family. Disturbed by the loss of her former friends and being unable to bear the situation in the village any longer, the girl killed herself by taking prussic acid, which she had stolen from her father's laboratory. At the inquest, the vicar attempted to blame the parishioners for his daughter's death but the coroner advised the jury to return a verdict of insufficient evidence. The resulting scandal reached the national press and the parishioners tried, unsuccessfully, to make amends by returning to church.

In 1911 Bryant married a lady who had answered his advertisement in the *Morning Post* for the position of housekeeper at the vicarage. This marriage was even more violent than his first and after three years of hostilities he locked his wife in her bedroom and went off to the church to conduct a service.

This very ordinary headstone in Stoke Lyne churchyard marks the burial place of Emily Ermyntrude Bryant. (Newsquest Oxfordshire)

The second Mrs Bryant, who escaped by jumping out of the window, brought an action against him for aggravated assault. Bicester magistrates issued a separation order and fined Bryant £10, which resulted in his being deprived of his living under the Clergy Discipline Act. He launched an appeal which was unsuccessful and the day after he found this out he went into a Bicester grocer's, where he bought a pound of sausages and then asked the shop owner and his assistant to witness his signature. What they had witnessed turned out to be Bryant's will naming his wife as executrix and sole beneficiary. Three days later he was found in a darkened room in the vicarage with a bullet through the head and a revolver in his hand. After a verdict of suicide was pronounced he was buried in his own churchyard. The register reads, 'This burial took place without the service of the Church of England. The service authorised for use in the Diocese was said'; a twentieth-century way of dealing with a suicide.

Alistair Grahame, the fortunate child whose father gave the world Rat, Mole, Toad and Badger, grew up to become an undergraduate at Christ Church. He died in 1920 when he threw himself under a train near Port Meadow. Father and son are buried in one grave in Oxford's Holywell cemetery. Their grave is to the right of the pathway on entering the cemetery; Kenneth's epitaph is on the nearside of the gravestone, Alistair's on the reverse. In the epitaph, Anthony Hope Hawkins says that Alistair, who was buried on his birthday, had 'now crossed the river'.

An example of the life-and-death effect that harsh weather conditions could have on those with inadequate shelter is given by Anthony Wood, who notes for 22 December 1679:

> extreame cold weather. A poore man died with hunger and cold: he began to die in St Clement's parish but the parishioners discovering it, hired or rather carried him under Magd. Tower in St Peter's parish East to die there and so save the parish 2 or 3 shillings to burye him.

The burial register of St Peter in the East does indeed record that on 24 December that year; 'A traveller whose name was not known' was buried in the churchyard.

A tragedy which shook the village of Stanton Harcourt in 1718 is recorded in a letter written by the poet Alexander Pope, who was staying at the manor at the time. It concerns John Hewit and Sarah Drew, a couple from the village who were struck by lightning while taking refuge from a storm by sheltering under a tree.

Only that morning John had obtained Sarah's father's permission for them to get married, so this was the first day of their engagement.

Then there was, writes Pope, 'so loud a crack, as if the heavens had burst asunder.' When the villagers went to look for the lovers, 'They saw a little smoke, and after, this faithful pair – John with one arm about his Sarah's neck, and the other held over her face, as if to screen her from the lightning. They were dead!' he adds. John and Sarah were buried the next day in the same grave and Lord Harcourt, at Popes suggestion, erected a monument in their memory, on which the poet wrote an epitaph which reads:

> Virtue unmoved can hear the call
> And face the flash that melts the ball.

A similar incident took place not that far away at Clanfield on 4 August 1843 and is marked by a stone set into the tower of the church. James Joy and Robert Cross were working in the fields when they were struck and killed by lightening.

The careless, or simply unlucky, sometimes lost their lives in drowning accidents. In 1627 at Thame two children by the names of Hambledon and Smart were drowned on 1 July. Both St Sepulchre's and Holywell cemeteries contain several examples of persons who met their deaths by drowning.

A small number of memorials in Oxfordshire are to those who died overseas and it is not always clear whether or not their bodies, or their ashes, are buried in the vicinity. This memorial to Bert Cooper in Holywell cemetery states that he was accidentally killed in Maritzburgh, South Africa in September 1903, when he was 24. Bert Cooper was a common enough name for a young man of his generation but this particular Bert was the son of Frank and Sarah of marmalade fame, whose former premises in Oxford High Street bears one of the city's few blue plaques.

Lightning victims at Stanton Harcourt. (Newsquest Oxfordshire)

A casket-tomb in Holywell cemetery commemorates 'Theodore and Sibley', a boy and his nurse maid, drowned near Medley. The register tells us that Elizabeth Sibley was aged 30 when she, and her charge Louis Theodore, the 4-year-old son of Giles Theodore and Margaretta Pilcher of 3 Norham Gardens, were buried on 3 June 1893.

In St Sepulchre's lie four young persons, two boys and two girls, who never came home after going out on a boat trip in 1854. They were drowned in the River Isis on 23 June 'by the accidental upsetting of a boat.' An identical accident had claimed the life of Exeter College undergraduate William Hender Gillbee, who was aged only twenty when the boat he was in was upset in 1851.

A brass inscription on the wall of Cuddesdon church reads:

> In loving memory of Alan John Martin, a chorister of this church, and of Edward Thomas Pinson, curate of this parish, who did not fear to face death as he tried to save the lad's life. They died together in the waters of the Thame; their bodies lie in one grave near this church.

This tragedy took place in 1903.

The casket-tomb in Holywell cemetery.

Some accidents, however, are caused more by reckless behaviour than forces of nature or Acts of God.

The inscription on the best-kept stone in St Sepulchre's cemetery states that Francis L.C. Tayler was the 'dearly loved husband of Phyllis, who sacrificed his life in the fulfilment of his duty.' Not a member of the armed forces or the emergency services as the wording suggests, Frankie Tayler was in fact a mechanic with the MG racing team based in Abingdon. He died in 1935 on the Isle of Man while a passenger in a racing car driven by wealthy socialite Kaye Don, who was later jailed for manslaughter. Tayler was only 28 and had been married less than a year. He had promised his wife Phyllis to give up motor-racing because it was too dangerous. Phyllis Tayler outlived her husband by sixty-six years, but never forgot him and her ashes were interred in the same grave in May 2000. The attractive gravestone has an Art Deco design which shows a racing car being driven into the sunset.

Most of Oxfordshire's larger towns and villages were badly affected by the cholera epidemics which swept the country in the nineteenth century. The principal outbreaks were in 1832, when ninety-five people died, in 1849 with seventy-five deaths, and in 1854, with 115 deaths from the disease in Oxford alone. The great majority of the cases came from St Clement's, St Thomas's (which at that time also included Jericho), and St Ebbe's parishes. These epidemics, together with frequent

Francis L.C. Tayler's gravestone in St Sepulchre's cemetery.

outbreaks of typhoid, typhus, measles and the ever-present tuberculosis, put extreme pressure on the space available for burials. As most of these were regarded by the Victorians as 'filth diseases', victims were not always accorded the compassion they might normally have received.

In Oxford, throughout the epidemic, litter-bearers and porters undertook some of the hardest and most harrowing work, for not only were they responsible for conveying patients to and from the convalescent house or hospital, they usually doubled-up as coffin-bearers, and were also involved in laying-out the dead and carrying them to the grave. For litter-bearing and porterage they received 2*s* 6*d* per bearer, with a weekly wage of 15*s* for those so engaged. Coffin-bearers received 15*s* a week each, while the rate for laying-out and accompanying to the grave was 5*s* for each funeral. Funeral expenses chargeable to the parish normally included brandy, beer, and tobacco for those directly involved in disposing of the corpse, while the cost of sufficient linen for a shroud was 7*d*.

The parish of St Peter le Bailey provides a good example of the cost of a complete funeral in 1832, that of William Cantwell, who was not himself a cholera victim. The sum of 9*s* 6*d* went to the minister officiating, 1*s* to the parish clerk, 1*s* for the passing bell, 3*s* for the grave, 1*s* for cords and boards, and 1*s* for turfing the grave. In St Thomas's, 'brandy for 10 funerals with cholera' from 2 July to 4 August, cost 5*s*; the carpenter, Henry Sides, received £1 5*s* for a black coffin from St Aldate's parish, and in St Clement's, funerals were charged at either 7*s* 6d or 5*s* 6*d*, with at cost of 2*s* for burying 'Lewis's stillborn'.

One unconventional expense was incurred when two cholera victims were taken punting at a cost of 3*s* 6*d*. A letter from John Walton, Beadle of the United Parishes, states that the bodies of Robert Stone and Sarah Cheeseman, who had died in the workhouse in Wellington Square, were taken down the canal in a punt as far as the Turnpike Bridge on the Botley Road, 'and from there down Kite Lane to the back of the Church thereby avoiding any crowd of persons that might be congregated together in the parish of St Thomas.'

The bodies of many cholera victims were put into mass graves, the exact locations of which remain uncertain in many cases but in the churchyard at Bicester, however, is a cholera stone which reads:

> ERECTED AT THE PUBLIC EXPENSE
> to the memory of
> Sixty four persons of this parish
> By CHOLERA MORBUS
> AD MDCCCXXXII
> Their Names are under written
> These Persons all died within the space of two months.

Those who died during the 1832 cholera epidemic at Wantage are not forgotten either for there is a memorial plaque on the wall of the parish church. This was restored in November 1960 and reads:

> Between this wall and the pathway were interred from September 29th to October 13th 1832, the bodies of sixteen persons, who, with three others of this Town had died of the Asiatic Cholera, the ravages of which disease were mercifully terminated by Him who alone could say to the Angel of the Pestilence, 'It is enough, stay now thine hand.'

In October 1965 a number of bones were disturbed by workmen trying to repair a burst water pipe on the wall of Wantage parish church. The *Oxford Times* reported that, 'None of the men was anxious to speculate whether they were those of the cholera victims. Nor would any of them be photographed.' (Newsquest Oxfordshire)

A corner of the older part of the Victorian cemetery in Abingdon is full of the graves of those who died during the influenza epidemic which followed the end of the First World War. There are no markers to be seen, but the area has been turned into a haven for wildlife.

Bibliography

Jackson's Oxford Journal, various years

Mee, A., *The King's England, Oxfordshire*, 1965

Newsquest Oxfordshire Group, various publications, various dates

Pevsner, N., *The Buildings of England, Berkshire*, 1966

Pevsner N. and Sherwood, J., (eds) *The Buildings of England, Oxfordshire*, 1974 edition

Victoria County History of Oxfordshire, various volumes

Wood, Anthony, (ed. Clark, A.) *Life and Times*, OUP, 1961

Other titles published by The History Press

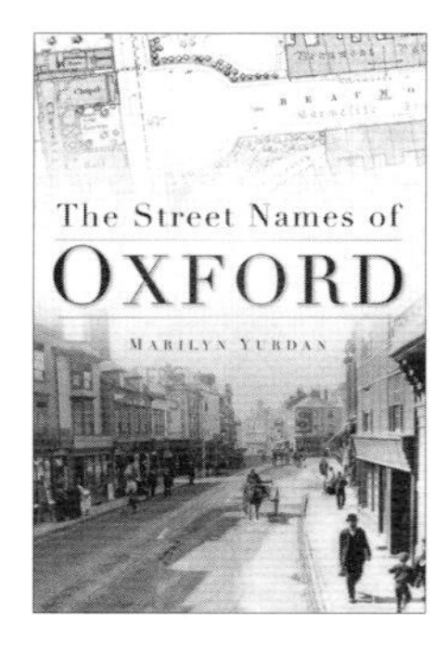

The Street Names of Oxford

MARILYN YURDAN

This book traces the origins of names found in Oxford, not only of its streets, villages, suburbs and housing estates, but also of the various colleges which make up the university, many of which have had a considerable influence on its streets. Containing illustrations that range in date from nineteenth-century prints to photographs of modern developments, this book is a must-read for everyone interested in Oxford's development.

978 0 7509 5098 5

Oxford in the 1950s & '60s

MARILYN YURDAN

Oxford in the 1950s & '60s offers a rare glimpse of life in the city during this fascinating period. As this amazing collection of 200 photographs shows, there is much more to these two decades than pop groups and mini skirts. Including views of Oxford's streets and buildings, shops and businesses, pubs and hotels, the Colleges and University departments, as well as some of the villages which form the suburbs of the city, this book is sure to appeal to all who remember these decades and everyone who knows and loves Oxford.

978 0 7524 5219 7

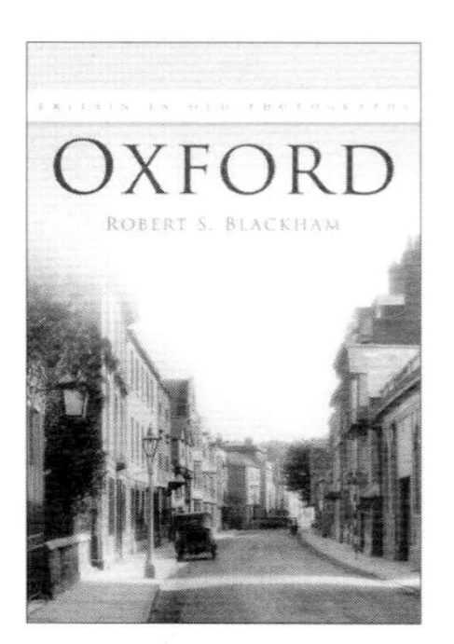

Oxford

ROBERT S. BLACKHAM

This selection of photographs and postcards provides a comprehensive guide to Oxford's past, using rare images of the city to bring a bygone era to life. Many of Oxford's celebrated landmarks, including the famous university buildings and the historic Broad Street, are fully explored by over 200 pictures. These are accompanied by informative captions which provide little-known information about the characters responsible for the development of Oxford up until the present day.

978 0 7524 5128 2

Oxford Then & Now

MALCOLM GRAHAM AND LAURENCE WATERS

Henry Taunt was Oxford's first commercial photographer, and the historical value of his work has long been recognised. This book includes just over 100 of his finest images, which are compared and contrasted with the scene today. Malcolm Graham, author of Taunt's biography and Oxford's best-known local historian, provides a knowledgeable and illuminating text, while the modern photographs have been specially taken for this book by Laurence Waters.

978 0 7509 4224 9